TRUMP TWEETS

THE COFFEE TABLE BOOK

Donald J. Trump ✔ @realDonaldTrump · Jan 17

A tremendous collection of **YOUR FAVORITE PRESIDENT'S BEST TWEETS** -- organized by topic! Even the haters and losers will wish they owned it. This book is a must-buy!

💬 7.9k   🔁 13k   ♡ 47k

FREE TRUMP TWEETS PUZZLES!

Write an honest review of this book on Amazon and send a screenshot of your posted review to **amusementsharkpublishing@gmail.com.** We'll reply with some of our fun Trump Tweets word search puzzles you can print at home! (Bonus points — and extra goodies! — if you include photos in your review.)

AMUSEMENT SHARK PUBLISHING

TABLE OF CONTENTS

TRUMP TWEETS ABOUT...

...TRUMP
4 "Trump"
5 Your Favorite President, Me!
6 I Was Right
7 Presidential Harassment
8 The Least Racist Person
9 A Very Stable Genius
10 More Than Any President
11 A "Tiny" Bit of Exercise
12 Ratings & Reviews
13 Thank You President Trump

...HIS PRESIDENCY
14 The 2016 Election
15 Make America Great Again
16 The Travel Ban
17 Rocket Man
18 The Wall is The Wall
19 Protests & Protesters
20 Witch Hunt!
21 Mar-a-Lago
22 The Supreme Court
23 Good Old Global Warming
24 A Very Big, Boring Bust
25 The Deep State
26 Space Force!
27 The Woodward Books
28 Hurricanes
29 My Friend Kim Jong Un
30 The California Wildfires
31 The Federal Reserve
32 A Perfect Phone Call
33 The Whistleblowers
34 Professional Sports
35 Former White House Officials
36 More Former White House Officials
37 The China Virus
38 The U.S. Postal System
39 Republican Leadership
40 The 2020 Election
41 The Final Tweets

...DEMOCRATS
42 The Do Nothing Party
43 Crooked Hillary Clinton
44 Former President Obama
45 Shifty Liddle' Adam Schiff
46 Nervous Nancy Pelosi
47 Cryin' Chuck Schumer
48 The Squad
49 Pocahontas
50 Crazy Bernie Sanders
51 Sleepy Joe Biden
52 A Socialist Nightmare
53 The 2020 Democratic Primary
54 Joe Biden's Basement

...REPUBLICANS
55 Our Great First Lady
56 Jared & Ivanka
57 Paul Ryan
58 Jeff Flake & Bob Corker
59 Mitt Romney
60 Michael Cohen
61 Jeff Sessions
62 Roger Stone
63 Rudy Giuliani
64 Paul Manafort
65 Brett Kavanaugh
66 The Mooch
67 Ben Sasse
68 John Bolton

...THE HATERS
09 Trump Haters
70 Losers
71 Lightweights
72 Clowns
73 Never Trumpers
74 Low IQ Individuals
75 Fools & Foolishness
76 Psychos
77 Lowlifes
78 Disasters
79 RINOs
80 The Dumbest
81 The Worst
82 The So-Called
83 Nicknames, Puns & Insults
84 Celebrity Feuds
85 More Celebrity Feuds
86 Social Media Giants
87 Big Tech

...THE MEDIA
88 The Real Opposition Party
89 The Enemy of The People
90 The Lamestream Media
91 Fake News!
92 More Fake News
93 Even More Fake News!
94 The Amazon Washington Post
95 The Failing New York Times
96 Fake News CNN
97 What's With Fox News?
98 We All Miss Roger Ailes
99 Return The Pulitzers!
100 Third-Rate Reporters
101 Freedom of the Press
102 Free Speech
103 Very Low Ratings

"TRUMP"

International businessman and former reality tv star Donald J. Trump was inaugurated as the 45th president of the United States on January 20, 2017 after receiving 304 electoral college votes in the 2016 election. He served as president until January 20, 2021, and, as part of his unique Twitter style, he often put his name in quotation marks when tweeting about himself.

Donald J. Trump ✓ @realDonaldTrump · Jan 10, 2019

There is GREAT unity with the Republicans in the House and Senate, despite the Fake News Media working in overdrive to make the story look otherwise. The Opposition Party & the Dems know we must have Strong Border Security, but don't want to give "Trump" another one of many wins!

Donald J. Trump ✓ @realDonaldTrump · Mar 2, 2019

Virtually everything failed lawyer Michael Cohen said in his sworn testimony last week is totally contradicted in his just released manuscript for a book about me. It's a total new love letter to "Trump" and the pols must now use it rather than his lies for sentence reduction!

Donald J. Trump ✓ @realDonaldTrump · Aug 8, 2019

I am so amazed that MSNBC & CNN can keep putting on, over and over again, people that have no idea what I am all about, and yet they speak as experts on "Trump." Same people since long before the 2016 Election, and how did that work out for the Haters and Losers. Not well!

Donald J. Trump ✓ @realDonaldTrump · Jun 1, 2020

"Trump" is leading in all swing states. Heavily biased Democrat Poll, just like 2016. Biggest "enthusiasm" lead ever!

Donald J. Trump ✓ @realDonaldTrump · Dec 29, 2020

The consent decree signed by the "Secretary", with the consent of Kemp, is perhaps even more poorly negotiated than the deal that John Kerry made with Iran. Now it turns out that Brad R's brother works for China, and they definitely don't want "Trump". So disgusting! #MAGA

YOUR FAVORITE PRESIDENT, ME!

President Trump rode a wave of red baseball caps across the Midwest, the Great Lakes, and the Southeast. It was that enthusiasm among the voters he often referred to as the "forgotten men and women of our country" that carried him all the way to the White House. On Twitter, the president was fond of reminding others of his popularity among his political supporters.

Donald J. Trump ✔ @realDonaldTrump · Jan 19, 2019

.@newtgingrich just stated that there has been no president since Abraham Lincoln who has been treated worse or more unfairly by the media than your favorite President, me! At the same time there has been no president who has accomplished more in his first two years in office!

Donald J. Trump ✔ @realDonaldTrump · Feb 24, 2019

HOLD THE DATE! We will be having one of the biggest gatherings in the history of Washington, D.C., on July 4th. It will be called "A Salute To America" and will be held at the Lincoln Memorial. Major fireworks display, entertainment and an address by your favorite President, me!

Donald J. Trump ✔ @realDonaldTrump · Aug 31, 2019

Has anyone noticed that the top shows on @foxnews and cable ratings are those that are Fair (or great) to your favorite President, me! Congratulations to @ seanhannity for being the number one show on Cable Television!

Donald J. Trump ✔ @realDonaldTrump · May 9, 2020

Why is it that all of the political pundits & consultants that I beat so easily & badly, people that charged their clients far more than their services were worth, have become so totally "unhinged" when it come to your favorite President, me. These people are stone cold crazy!

Donald J. Trump ✔ @realDonaldTrump · Nov 1, 2020

Chris Wallace of @FoxNews, by far the lowest rated of the Sunday morning news programs, can't get over his poor debate performance, probably even worse than Sleepy Joe's. His show is a total "hit job" on your favorite President, me!

I WAS RIGHT

As the most unconventional leader of the free world in recent memory, President Trump faced a whirlwind of criticism. Democrats, the mainstream media, and a handful of Republicans denounced his use of Twitter, his norm-shattering policy decisions, and pretty much everything he ever said — so he was quick to claim vindication whenever he felt he was proven correct.

Donald J. Trump ✔ @realDonaldTrump · Nov 3, 2017

I always felt I would be running and winning against Bernie Sanders, not Crooked H, without cheating, I was right.

Donald J. Trump ✔ @realDonaldTrump · Jul 26, 2020

Crazy Nancy Pelosi said I made a mistake when I banned people from infected China from entering the U.S. in January. Tens of thousands of lives were saved, as she danced in the Streets of Chinatown (SF) in late February. Biden agreed with her, but soon admitted that I was right!

Donald J. Trump ✔ @realDonaldTrump · Sep 13, 2020

I was right, these people were all wrong, and now they criticize me. Such hypocrisy!

Donald J. Trump ✔ @realDonaldTrump · Oct 12, 2020

The World Health Organization just admitted that I was right. Lockdowns are killing countries all over the world. The cure cannot be worse than the problem itself. Open up your states, Democrat governors. Open up New York. A long battle, but they finally did the right thing!

Donald J. Trump ✔ @realDonaldTrump · Oct 15, 2020

I was right again! Steve Scully just admitted he was lying about his Twitter being hacked. The Debate was Rigged! He was suspended from @cspan indefinitely. The Trump Campaign was not treated fairly by the "Commission". Did I show good instincts in being the first to know?

PRESIDENTIAL HARASSMENT

President Trump was the subject of numerous, as he tweeted it, "witch hunts." Of those witch hunts, he tweeted most often about the Special Counsel investigation into Russian interference in the 2016 election. During his four years in the White House, he published a tweet that read simply "PRESIDENTIAL HARASSMENT!" in all caps 13 times (and another four times not in all caps).

Donald J. Trump ✔ @realDonaldTrump · Nov 12, 2018

The prospect of Presidential Harassment by the Dems is causing the Stock Market big headaches!

Donald J. Trump ✔ @realDonaldTrump · Dec 6, 2018

Without the phony Russia Witch Hunt, and with all that we have accomplished in the last almost two years (Tax & Regulation Cuts, Judge's, Military, Vets, etc.) my approval rating would be at 75% rather than the 50% just reported by Rasmussen. It's called Presidential Harassment!

Donald J. Trump ✔ @realDonaldTrump · May 30, 2019

So now Congressman Adam Schiff announces, after having found zero Russian Collusion, that he is going to be looking at every aspect of my life, both financial and personal, even though there is no reason to be doing so. Never happened before! Unlimited Presidential Harassment

Donald J. Trump ✔ @realDonaldTrump · May 30, 2019

The Greatest Presidential Harassment in history. After spending $40,000,000 over two dark years, with unlimited access, people, resources and cooperation, highly conflicted Robert Mueller would have brought charges, if he had ANYTHING, but there were no charges to bring!

Donald J. Trump ✔ @realDonaldTrump · Jan 9, 2020

Hope that all House Republicans will vote against Crazy Nancy Pelosi's War Powers Resolution. Also, remember her "speed & rush" in getting the Impeachment Hoax voted on & done. Well, she never sent the Articles to the Senate. Just another Democrat fraud. Presidential Harassment!

THE LEAST RACIST PERSON

President Trump, who tweeted his opinion of just about everyone and everything, was publicly accused multiple times throughout his presidency of being a racist. In response to those accusations, the president frequently referenced his administration's employment statistics, which showed Black, Hispanic, and Asian unemployment at their lowest since the 1960s and 1970s.

Donald J. Trump ✔ @realDonaldTrump · Jul 16, 2019

Those Tweets were NOT Racist. I don't have a Racist bone in my body! The so-called vote to be taken is a Democrat con game. Republicans should not show "weakness" and fall into their trap. This should be a vote on the filthy language, statements and lies told by the Democrat Congresswomen.

Donald J. Trump ✔ @realDonaldTrump · Jul 28, 2019

There is nothing racist in stating plainly what most people already know, that Elijah Cummings has done a terrible job for the people of his district, and of Baltimore itself. Dems always play the race card when they are unable to win with facts. Shame!

Donald J. Trump ✔ @realDonaldTrump · Jul 31, 2019

CNN's Don Lemon, the dumbest man on television, insinuated last night while asking a debate "question" that I was a racist, when in fact I am "the least racist person in the world." Perhaps someone should explain to Don that he is supposed to be neutral, unbiased & fair.

Donald J. Trump ✔ @realDonaldTrump · Aug 6, 2019

"It's political season and the election is around the corner. They want to continue to push that racist narrative." @ainsleyearhardt @foxandfriends And I am the least racist person. Black, Hispanic and Asian Unemployment is the lowest (BEST) in the history of the United States!

Donald J. Trump ✔ @realDonaldTrump · Sep 2, 2019

The Amazon Washington Post did a story that I brought racist attacks against the "Squad." No, they brought racist attacks against our Nation. All I do is call them out for the horrible things they have said. The Democrats have become the Party of the Squad!

A VERY STABLE GENIUS

Following the release of "Fire and Fury" by Michael Wolff, which painted an unflattering portrait of the president as unintelligent, ill-prepared, and mentally unfit for his leadership position, President Trump took to Twitter to defend himself. He dubbed himself a "very stable genius" and was instantly mocked online. The president, however, embraced the phrase and continued to use it.

Donald J. Trump @realDonaldTrump · Jan 6, 2018

Actually, throughout my life, my two greatest assets have been mental stability and being, like, really smart. Crooked Hillary Clinton also played these cards very hard and, as everyone knows, went down in flames. I went from VERY successful businessman, to top T.V. Star.....

Donald J. Trump @realDonaldTrump · Jan 6, 2018

....to President of the United States (on my first try). I think that would qualify as not smart, but genius....and a very stable genius at that!

Donald J. Trump @realDonaldTrump · Jul 11, 2019

Could you imagine having Sleepy Joe Biden, or @AlfredENeuman99, or a very nervous and skinny version of Pocahontas (1/1024th), as your President, rather than what you have now, so great looking and smart, a true Stable Genius! Sorry to say that even Social Media would be driven out of business.

Donald J. Trump @realDonaldTrump · Sep 14, 2019

"A Very Stable Genius!" Thank you.

Donald J. Trump @realDonaldTrump · Oct 14, 2019

Former Democrat Senator Harry Reid just stated that Donald Trump is very smart, much more popular than people think, is underestimated, and will be hard to beat in the 2020 Election. Thank you Harry, I agree!

MORE THAN ANY PRESIDENT

Studies have shown that there was very little positive press coverage of President Trump during his time in the White House. Rather than relying on long-established outlets like The New York Times and The Washington Post to applaud his achievements, President Trump instead took to Twitter to remind the American people of the things his administration had accomplished.

Donald J. Trump ✔ @realDonaldTrump · Dec 23, 2017

The Stock Market is setting record after record and unemployment is at a 17 year low. So many things accomplished by the Trump Administration, perhaps more than any other President in first year. Sadly, will never be reported correctly by the Fake News Media!

Donald J. Trump ✔ @realDonaldTrump · Jun 4, 2018

This is my 500th. Day in Office and we have accomplished a lot - many believe more than any President in his first 500 days. Massive Tax & Regulation Cuts, Military & Vets, Lower Crime & Illegal Immigration, Stronger Borders, Judgeships, Best Economy & Jobs EVER, and much more.

Donald J. Trump ✔ @realDonaldTrump · Jan 4, 2019

How do you impeach a president who has won perhaps the greatest election of all time, done nothing wrong (no Collusion with Russia, it was the Dems that Colluded), had the most successful first two years of any president, and is the most popular Republican in party history 93%?

Donald J. Trump ✔ @realDonaldTrump · Sep 9, 2019

The Trump Administration has achieved more in the first 2 1/2 years of its existence than perhaps any administration in the history of our Country. We get ZERO media credit for what we have done, and are doing, but the people know, and that's all that is important!

Donald J. Trump ✔ @realDonaldTrump · Jan 28, 2020

It's amazing what I've done, the most of any President in the first three years (by far), considering that for three years I've been under phony political investigations and the Impeachment Hoax! KEEP AMERICA GREAT!

A "TINY" BIT OF EXERCISE

President Trump played approximately 300 rounds of golf, the preferred physical activity of many presidents, during his four years in Washington. For historical context, during their eight-year presidencies, former President Obama played 330 rounds of golf, President Eisenhower played 800 rounds of golf, and President Wilson played an incredible 1,200 rounds of golf.

Donald J. Trump ✔ @realDonaldTrump · Jul 14, 2018

I have arrived in Scotland and will be at Trump Turnberry for two days of meetings, calls and hopefully, some golf - my primary form of exercise! The weather is beautiful, and this place is incredible! Tomorrow I go to Helsinki for a Monday meeting with Vladimir Putin.

Donald J. Trump ✔ @realDonaldTrump · May 24, 2020

Sleepy Joe's representatives have just put out an ad saying that I went to play golf (exercise) today. They think I should stay in the White House at all times. What they didn't say is that it's the first time I've played golf in almost 3 months, that Biden was constantly vacationing, relaxing & making shady deals with other countries.

Donald J. Trump ✔ @realDonaldTrump · May 25, 2020

Some stories about the fact that in order to get outside and perhaps, even a little exercise, I played golf over the weekend. The Fake & Totally Corrupt News makes it sound like a mortal sin - I knew this would happen! What they don't say is that it was my first golf in almost 3 months.

Donald J. Trump ✔ @realDonaldTrump · Jul 12, 2020

I know many in business and politics that work out endlessly, in some cases to a point of exhaustion. It is their number one passion in life, but nobody complains. My "exercise" is playing, almost never during the week, a quick round of golf. Obama played more and much longer....

Donald J. Trump ✔ @realDonaldTrump · Jul 12, 2020

...rounds, no problem. When I play, Fake News CNN, and others, park themselves anywhere they can to get a picture, then scream "President Trump is playing golf." Actually, I play VERY fast, get a lot of work done on the golf course, and also get a "tiny" bit of exercise. Not bad!

RATINGS & REVIEWS

President Trump was a mega ratings booster for mainstream media outlets like Fox News, CNN, and MSNBC — and he didn't let them, or his Twitter followers, forget it. The president appeared particularly pleased after The New York Times described the number of viewers his press conferences drew in to those of Monday Night Football and the reality tv series The Bachelor.

Donald J. Trump ✔ @realDonaldTrump · Feb 1, 2018

Thank you for all of the nice compliments and reviews on the State of the Union speech. 45.6 million people watched, the highest number in history. @FoxNews beat every other Network, for the first time ever, with 11.7 million people tuning in. Delivered from the heart!

Donald J. Trump ✔ @realDonaldTrump · Mar 29, 2020

Because the "Ratings" of my News Conferences etc. are so high, "Bachelor finale, Monday Night Football type numbers" according to the @nytimes, the Lamestream Media is going CRAZY. "Trump is reaching too many people, we must stop him." said one lunatic. See you at 5:00 P.M.!

Donald J. Trump ✔ @realDonaldTrump · Apr 21, 2020

I've had great "ratings" my whole life, there's nothing unusual about that for me. The White House News Conference ratings are "through the roof"(Monday Night Football, Bachelor Finale , @nytimes) but I don't care about that. I care about going around the Fake News to the PEOPLE!

Donald J. Trump ✔ @realDonaldTrump · Jun 27, 2020

Do not believe the Fake News Media. Oklahoma speech had the highest Saturday television ratings in @FoxNews history. @seanhannity dominated T.V. with my interview on Thursday night, more than @CNN & MSDNC COMBINED. These are the real polls, the Silent Majority, not FAKE POLLS!

Donald J. Trump ✔ @realDonaldTrump · Sep 30, 2020

HIGHEST CABLE TELEVISION RATINGS OF ALL TIME. SECOND HIGHEST OVERALL TELEVISION RATINGS OF ALL TIME. Some day these Fake Media Companies are going to miss me, very badly!!!

THANK YOU PRESIDENT TRUMP

When the press didn't applaud him for the things he thought he deserved to be thanked for, President Trump took praising himself into his own hands. He publicly thanked himself on Twitter for everything from leaps in television ratings to other people's failed presidential campaigns. His tweets brought a whole new meaning to the inspirational saying "Be your own biggest fan."

Donald J. Trump ✔ @realDonaldTrump · May 13, 2019

Also, congratulations to @OANN on the great job you are doing and the big ratings jump ("thank you President Trump")!

Donald J. Trump ✔ @realDonaldTrump · Jun 2, 2020

D.C. had no problems last night. Many arrests. Great job done by all. Overwhelming force. Domination. Likewise, Minneapolis was great (thank you President Trump!).

Donald J. Trump ✔ @realDonaldTrump · Jun 25, 2020

Failed presidential candidate (thank you President Trump!), Carly Fiorina, said she will be voting for Corrupt Joe Biden. She lost so badly to me, twice in one campaign, that she should be voting for Joe. No complaints!!!

Donald J. Trump ✔ @realDonaldTrump · Jul 1, 2020

Can't believe how badly @CNN has done in the newly released TV ratings. They are so far below @FoxNews (thank you President Trump!) that you can barely find them. Fredo should be given a big pay cut! MSDNC also did poorly. As I have long said, Fake News does not pay!!!

Donald J. Trump ✔ @realDonaldTrump · Aug 13, 2020

Very poor morning TV ratings for MSDNC's Morning Joe, headed by a complete Psycho named Joe Scarborough and his ditzy airhead wife, Mika, and also @CNN, headed by complete unknowns. Congratulations to @foxandfriends on dominating the mornings (thank you President Trump!).

THE 2016 ELECTION

Following a controversial presidential campaign during which he ridiculed Republican candidates, asked his rally attendees to "knock the crap out of" protesters and offered to pay the resulting legal fees, and promised that Mexico would pay for a Southern border wall, Donald J. Trump shocked pollsters by winning the 2016 election — and he reminisced about that feat on Twitter.

Donald J. Trump ✔ @realDonaldTrump · Nov 9, 2018

In the 2016 Election I was winning by so much in Florida that Broward County, which was very late with vote tabulation and probably getting ready to do a "number," couldn't do it because not enough people live in Broward for them to falsify a victory!

Donald J. Trump ✔ @realDonaldTrump · Jan 24, 2019

A great new book just out, "Game of Thorns," by Doug Wead, Presidential Historian and best selling author. The book covers the campaign of 2016, and what could be more exciting than that?

Donald J. Trump ✔ @realDonaldTrump · Apr 13, 2019

When I won the Election in 2016, the @nytimes had to beg their fleeing subscribers for forgiveness in that they covered the Election (and me) so badly. They didn't have a clue, it was pathetic. They even apologized to me. But now they are even worse, really corrupt reporting!

Donald J. Trump ✔ @realDonaldTrump · May 11, 2019

I won the 2016 Election partially based on no Tax Returns while I am under audit (which I still am), and the voters didn't care. Now the Radical Left Democrats want to again relitigate this matter. Make it a part of the 2020 Election!

Donald J. Trump ✔ @realDonaldTrump · Aug 19, 2019

Wow, Report Just Out! Google manipulated from 2.6 million to 16 million votes for Hillary Clinton in 2016 Election! This was put out by a Clinton supporter, not a Trump Supporter! Google should be sued. My victory was even bigger than thought! @JudicialWatch

MAKE AMERICA GREAT AGAIN

Throughout his campaign and presidency, President Trump used the same slogan that helped carry Ronald Reagan to the White House in 1980: Make America Great Again, which he abbreviated to MAGA. Emblazoned in white on red hats across America, the slogan was updated to Keep America Great during the president's re-election campaign but MAGA remained popular.

Donald J. Trump ✔ @realDonaldTrump · Feb 25, 2017

Maybe the millions of people who voted to MAKE AMERICA GREAT AGAIN should have their own rally. It would be the biggest of them all!

Donald J. Trump ✔ @realDonaldTrump · Jul 1, 2017

My use of social media is not Presidential - it's MODERN DAY PRESIDENTIAL. Make America Great Again!

Donald J. Trump ✔ @realDonaldTrump · Dec 24, 2017

The Fake News refuses to talk about how Big and how Strong our BASE is. They show Fake Polls just like they report Fake News. Despite only negative reporting, we are doing well - nobody is going to beat us. MAKE AMERICA GREAT AGAIN!

Donald J. Trump ✔ @realDonaldTrump · Aug 29, 2018

Big Election Wins last night! The Republican Party will MAKE AMERICA GREAT AGAIN! Actually, it is happening faster than anybody thought possible! It is morphing into KEEP AMERICA GREAT!

Donald J. Trump ✔ @realDonaldTrump · Mar 5, 2019

Republican Approval Rating just hit 93%. Sorry Haters! MAKE AMERICA GREAT AGAIN!

THE TRAVEL BAN

After calling for a "total and complete shutdown of Muslims entering the United States" as a presidential candidate in 2015, President Trump used one of his first executive actions to restrict travel into the United States from seven predominantly Muslim countries. When the decision was criticized, he took to Twitter and doubled down on the controversial term "travel ban."

Donald J. Trump ✓ @realDonaldTrump · Feb 4, 2017

What is our country coming to when a judge can halt a Homeland Security travel ban and anyone, even with bad intentions, can come into U.S.?

Donald J. Trump ✓ @realDonaldTrump · Jun 3, 2017

We need to be smart, vigilant and tough. We need the courts to give us back our rights. We need the Travel Ban as an extra level of safety!

Donald J. Trump ✓ @realDonaldTrump · Jun 5, 2017

People, the lawyers and the courts can call it whatever they want, but I am calling it what we need and what it is, a TRAVEL BAN!

Donald J. Trump ✓ @realDonaldTrump · Jun 5, 2017

That's right, we need a TRAVEL BAN for certain DANGEROUS countries, not some politically correct term that won't help us protect our people!

Donald J. Trump ✓ @realDonaldTrump · Jun 26, 2018

SUPREME COURT UPHOLDS TRUMP TRAVEL BAN. Wow!

ROCKET MAN

President Trump addressed North Korea's leader, Kim Jong Un, as "Rocket Man" on the world stage during his first address to the United Nations in 2017, saying "Rocket Man is on a suicide mission." The nickname originated as a response to Kim Jong Un's obsession with developing nuclear missiles and the president often used it when tweeting about the communist leader.

Donald J. Trump ✔ @realDonaldTrump · Sep 17, 2017

I spoke with President Moon of South Korea last night. Asked him how Rocket Man is doing. Long gas lines forming in North Korea. Too bad!

Donald J. Trump ✔ @realDonaldTrump · Sep 23, 2017

Just heard Foreign Minister of North Korea speak at U.N. If he echoes thoughts of Little Rocket Man, they won't be around much longer!

Donald J. Trump ✔ @realDonaldTrump · Oct 1, 2017

Being nice to Rocket Man hasn't worked in 25 years, why would it work now? Clinton failed, Bush failed, and Obama failed. I won't fail.

Donald J. Trump ✔ @realDonaldTrump · Nov 11, 2017

Why would Kim Jong-un insult me by calling me "old," when I would NEVER call him "short and fat?" Oh well, I try so hard to be his friend - and maybe someday that will happen!

Donald J. Trump ✔ @realDonaldTrump · Jan 2, 2018

North Korean Leader Kim Jong Un just stated that the "Nuclear Button is on his desk at all times." Will someone from his depleted and food starved regime please inform him that I too have a Nuclear Button, but it is a much bigger & more powerful one than his, and my Button works!

THE WALL IS THE WALL

What began as a chant in crowded auditoriums across America ultimately became President Trump's signature policy issue: the border wall. By the end of his presidency, his administration had successfully replaced 365 miles of existing border fencing and constructed 40 miles of new barriers along the approximately 2,000-mile southern border between the U.S. and Mexico.

Donald J. Trump ✓ @realDonaldTrump · Jan 18, 2018

The Wall is the Wall, it has never changed or evolved from the first day I conceived of it. Parts will be, of necessity, see through and it was never intended to be built in areas where there is natural protection such as mountains, wastelands or tough rivers or water.

Donald J. Trump ✓ @realDonaldTrump · Jan 18, 2018

The Wall will be paid for, directly or indirectly, or through longer term reimbursement, by Mexico, which has a ridiculous $71 billion dollar trade surplus with the U.S. The $20 billion dollar Wall is "peanuts" compared to what Mexico makes from the U.S. NAFTA is a bad joke!

Donald J. Trump ✓ @realDonaldTrump · Feb 23, 2018

MS-13 gang members are being removed by our Great ICE and Border Patrol Agents by the thousands, but these killers come back in from El Salvador, and through Mexico, like water. El Salvador just takes our money, and Mexico must help MORE with this problem. We need The Wall!

Donald J. Trump ✓ @realDonaldTrump · Dec 13, 2018

I often stated, "One way or the other, Mexico is going to pay for the Wall." This has never changed. Our new deal with Mexico (and Canada), the USMCA, is so much better than the old, very costly & anti-USA NAFTA deal, that just by the money we save, MEXICO IS PAYING FOR THE WALL!

Donald J. Trump ✓ @realDonaldTrump · Dec 31, 2018

An all concrete Wall was NEVER ABANDONED, as has been reported by the media. Some areas will be all concrete but the experts at Border Patrol prefer a Wall that is see through (thereby making it possible to see what is happening on both sides). Makes sense to me!

PROTESTS & PROTESTERS

Given the controversial nature of his campaign, it's no surprise that President Trump inspired the largest single-day protest in United States history. The Women's March, which took place on his first full day in the Oval Office, was the first of many protests related to the president, who repeatedly claimed on Twitter that anti-Trump protesters were actually paid actors.

Donald J. Trump ✔ @realDonaldTrump · Jan 22, 2017

Watched protests yesterday but was under the impression that we just had an election! Why didn't these people vote? Celebs hurt cause badly.

Donald J. Trump ✔ @realDonaldTrump · Feb 3, 2017

Professional anarchists, thugs and paid protesters are proving the point of the millions of people who voted to MAKE AMERICA GREAT AGAIN!

Donald J. Trump ✔ @realDonaldTrump · Oct 5, 2018

The very rude elevator screamers are paid professionals only looking to make Senators look bad. Don't fall for it! Also, look at all of the professionally made identical signs. Paid for by Soros and others. These are not signs made in the basement from love! #Troublemakers

Donald J. Trump ✔ @realDonaldTrump · Oct 9, 2018

The paid D.C. protesters are now ready to REALLY protest because they haven't gotten their checks - in other words, they weren't paid! Screamers in Congress, and outside, were far too obvious - less professional than anticipated by those paying (or not paying) the bills!

Donald J. Trump ✔ @realDonaldTrump · May 30, 2020

The professionally managed so-called "protesters" at the White House had little to do with the memory of George Floyd. They were just there to cause trouble. The @SecretService handled them easily. Tonight, I understand, is MAGA NIGHT AT THE WHITE HOUSE???

WITCH HUNT!

First and most frequently used to describe the Special Counsel investigation into Russian interference in the 2016 election, "witch hunt" also became President Trump's preferred term for the impeachment trial that resulted from his infamous phone call with the president of Ukraine. The president ultimately tweeted the phrase 351 times during his four years in Washington.

Donald J. Trump ✓ @realDonaldTrump · Jun 15, 2017

You are witnessing the single greatest WITCH HUNT in American political history - led by some very bad and conflicted people! #MAGA

Donald J. Trump ✓ @realDonaldTrump · Apr 30, 2018

The White House is running very smoothly despite phony Witch Hunts etc. There is great Energy and unending Stamina, both necessary to get things done. We are accomplishing the unthinkable and setting positive records while doing so! Fake News is going "bonkers!"

Donald J. Trump ✓ @realDonaldTrump · Jun 4, 2018

As has been stated by numerous legal scholars, I have the absolute right to PARDON myself, but why would I do that when I have done nothing wrong? In the meantime, the never ending Witch Hunt, led by 13 very Angry and Conflicted Democrats (& others) continues into the mid-terms!

Donald J. Trump ✓ @realDonaldTrump · Nov 29, 2018

When will this illegal Joseph McCarthy style Witch Hunt, one that has shattered so many innocent lives, ever end-or will it just go on forever? After wasting more than $40,000,000 (is that possible?), it has proven only one thing-there was NO Collusion with Russia. So Ridiculous!

Donald J. Trump ✓ @realDonaldTrump · Jan 26, 2019

WITCH HUNT!

MAR-A-LAGO

Although President Trump visited more than a dozen of his real estate properties during his presidency, his favorite by far was the Palm Beach resort he sometimes referred to as the Winter White House or Southern White House: Mar-a-Lago. The president spent nearly 140 days at the resort, where he hosted world leaders, played golf, and sometimes crashed weddings.

Donald J. Trump ✓ @realDonaldTrump · Feb 11, 2017

A working dinner tonight with Prime Minister Abe of Japan, and his representatives, at the Winter White House (Mar-a-Lago). Very good talks!

Donald J. Trump ✓ @realDonaldTrump · Feb 11, 2017

Melania and I are hosting Japanese Prime Minister Shinzo Abe and Mrs. Abe at Mar-a-Lago in Palm Beach, Fla. They are a wonderful couple!

Donald J. Trump ✓ @realDonaldTrump · Jun 29, 2017

I heard poorly rated @Morning_Joe speaks badly of me (don't watch anymore). Then how come low I.Q. Crazy Mika, along with Psycho Joe, came to Mar-a-Lago 3 nights in a row around New Year's Eve, and insisted on joining me. She was bleeding badly from a face-lift. I said no!

Donald J. Trump ✓ @realDonaldTrump · Nov 22, 2017

Will be having meetings and working the phones from the Winter White House in Florida (Mar-a-Lago). Stock Market hit new Record High yesterday - $5.5 trillion gain since E. Many companies coming back to the U.S. Military building up and getting very strong.

Donald J. Trump ✓ @realDonaldTrump · Apr 21, 2018

Heading to the Southern White House to watch the Funeral Service of Barbara Bush. First Lady Melania has arrived in Houston to pay our respects. Will be a beautiful day!

THE SUPREME COURT

During his four years in the White House, President Trump became the first president in 30 years to successfully nominate three justices to the Supreme Court: Justices Neil Gorsuch, Brett Kavanaugh, and Amy Coney Barrett. President Trump's nominees now make up one-third of the Supreme Court and will impact the judicial future of the United States for decades to come.

Donald J. Trump ✔ @realDonaldTrump · Dec 19, 2017

A story in the @washingtonpost that I was close to "rescinding" the nomination of Justice Gorsuch prior to confirmation is FAKE NEWS. I never even wavered and am very proud of him and the job he is doing as a Justice of the U.S. Supreme Court. The unnamed sources don't exist!

Donald J. Trump ✔ @realDonaldTrump · Sep 18, 2018

The Supreme Court is one of the main reasons I got elected President. I hope Republican Voters, and others, are watching, and studying, the Democrats Playbook.

Donald J. Trump ✔ @realDonaldTrump · Sep 28, 2018

Just started, tonight, our 7th FBI investigation of Judge Brett Kavanaugh. He will someday be recognized as a truly great Justice of The United States Supreme Court!

Donald J. Trump ✔ @realDonaldTrump · Jun 18, 2020

These horrible & politically charged decisions coming out of the Supreme Court are shotgun blasts into the face of people that are proud to call themselves Republicans or Conservatives. We need more Justices or we will lose our 2nd. Amendment & everything else. Vote Trump 2020!

Donald J. Trump ✔ @realDonaldTrump · Oct 27, 2020

Last night, we made history and confirmed Amy Coney Barrett to the United States Supreme Court! Justice Barrett will defend our rights, our liberties, and our God-Given FREEDOM!

GOOD OLD GLOBAL WARMING

Given his 2012 tweet that climate change was "created by and for the Chinese in order to make US manufacturing non-competitive," few were surprised when President Trump prioritized the economy over the environment. During his presidency, he delivered on his campaign promises to withdraw the U.S. from the Paris Agreement and approve the controversial Keystone XL pipeline.

Donald J. Trump ✔ @realDonaldTrump · Dec 28, 2017

In the East, it could be the COLDEST New Year's Eve on record. Perhaps we could use a little bit of that good old Global Warming that our Country, but not other countries, was going to pay TRILLIONS OF DOLLARS to protect against. Bundle up!

Donald J. Trump ✔ @realDonaldTrump · Nov 21, 2018

Brutal and Extended Cold Blast could shatter ALL RECORDS - Whatever happened to Global Warming?

Donald J. Trump ✔ @realDonaldTrump · Jan 20, 2019

Be careful and try staying in your house. Large parts of the Country are suffering from tremendous amounts of snow and near record setting cold. Amazing how big this system is. Wouldn't be bad to have a little of that good old fashioned Global Warming right now!

Donald J. Trump ✔ @realDonaldTrump · Jan 28, 2019

In the beautiful Midwest, windchill temperatures are reaching minus 60 degrees, the coldest ever recorded. In coming days, expected to get even colder. People can't last outside even for minutes. What the hell is going on with Global Waming? Please come back fast, we need you!

Donald J. Trump ✔ @realDonaldTrump · Feb 10, 2019

Well, it happened again. Amy Klobuchar announced that she is running for President, talking proudly of fighting global warming while standing in a virtual blizzard of snow, ice and freezing temperatures. Bad timing. By the end of her speech she looked like a Snowman(woman)!

A VERY BIG, BORING BUST

Breaking from tradition, President Trump opted not to attend the White House Correspondents' Dinner, an annual gathering of journalists, politicians, and celebrities. He became the first president to ever skip the dinner, often hosted by a well-known stand-up comedian who roasts the current president and other influential figures in attendance, every year of his presidency.

Donald J. Trump ✔ @realDonaldTrump · Feb 25, 2017

I will not be attending the White House Correspondents' Association Dinner this year. Please wish everyone well and have a great evening!

Donald J. Trump ✔ @realDonaldTrump · Apr 29, 2018

While Washington, Michigan, was a big success, Washington, D.C., just didn't work. Everyone is talking about the fact that the White House Correspondents Dinner was a very big, boring bust...the so-called comedian really "bombed." @greggutfeld should host next year! @PeteHegseth

Donald J. Trump ✔ @realDonaldTrump · Apr 29, 2018

The White House Correspondents' Dinner was a failure last year, but this year was an embarrassment to everyone associated with it. The filthy "comedian" totally bombed (couldn't even deliver her lines-much like the Seth Meyers weak performance). Put Dinner to rest, or start over!

Donald J. Trump ✔ @realDonaldTrump · Apr 30, 2018

The White House Correspondents' Dinner is DEAD as we know it. This was a total disaster and an embarrassment to our great Country and all that it stands for. FAKE NEWS is alive and well and beautifully represented on Saturday night!

Donald J. Trump ✔ @realDonaldTrump · Nov 20, 2018

So-called comedian Michelle Wolf bombed so badly last year at the White House Correspondents' Dinner that this year, for the first time in decades, they will have an author instead of a comedian. Good first step in comeback of a dying evening and tradition! Maybe I will go?

THE DEEP STATE

Toward the end of his first year in Washington, President Trump sent his first tweet alleging the existence of a "deep state" aka an organized resistance to his agenda within the government. Over the years, he blamed the Deep State for everything from the near-constant leaks coming from within his administration to the length of time it took the FDA to approve a covid vaccine.

Donald J. Trump ✔ @realDonaldTrump · Nov 28, 2017

Charles McCullough, the respected fmr Intel Comm Inspector General, said public was misled on Crooked Hillary Emails. "Emails endangered National Security." Why aren't our deep State authorities looking at this? Rigged & corrupt? @TuckerCarlson @seanhannity

Donald J. Trump ✔ @realDonaldTrump · Jul 14, 2018

Where is the DNC Server, and why didn't the FBI take possession of it? Deep State?

Donald J. Trump ✔ @realDonaldTrump · Sep 15, 2019

I am fighting the Fake (Corrupt) News, the Deep State, the Democrats, and the few remaining Republicans In Name Only (RINOS, who are on mouth to mouth resuscitation), with the help of some truly great Republicans, and others. We are Winning big (150th Federal Judge this week)!

Donald J. Trump ✔ @realDonaldTrump · Sep 21, 2019

Some of the best Economic Numbers our Country has ever experienced are happening right now. This is despite a Crooked and Demented Deep State, and a probably illegal Democrat/Fake News Media Partnership the likes of which the world has never seen. MAKE AMERICA GREAT AGAIN!

Donald J. Trump ✔ @realDonaldTrump · Aug 22, 2020

The deep state, or whoever, over at the FDA is making it very difficult for drug companies to get people in order to test the vaccines and therapeutics. Obviously, they are hoping to delay the answer until after November 3rd. Must focus on speed, and saving lives! @SteveFDA

SPACE FORCE!

With the swipe of his infamous black Sharpie, President Trump authorized the creation of the first new branch of the U.S. armed services in more than 70 years. Rather than focusing on Star Trek-like space exploration, the Space Force was created to protect American assets like GPS and communication satellites from foreign interference or attack while they are orbiting the earth.

Donald J. Trump ✔ @realDonaldTrump · Aug 3, 2018

NASA, which is making a BIG comeback under the Trump Administration, has just named 9 astronauts for Boeing and Spacex space flights. We have the greatest facilities in the world and we are now letting the private sector pay to use them. Exciting things happening. Space Force!

Donald J. Trump ✔ @realDonaldTrump · Aug 9, 2018

Space Force all the way!

Donald J. Trump ✔ @realDonaldTrump · Jun 7, 2019

For all of the money we are spending, NASA should NOT be talking about going to the Moon - We did that 50 years ago. They should be focused on the much bigger things we are doing, including Mars (of which the Moon is a part), Defense and Science!

Donald J. Trump ✔ @realDonaldTrump · Dec 9, 2019

.@NATO has now recognized SPACE as an operational domain and the alliance is STRONGER for it. U.S. leadership ensures peace through strength and we must continue to show strength and WIN on all fronts – land, air, sea, and SPACE!

Donald J. Trump ✔ @realDonaldTrump · Aug 5, 2020

NASA was Closed & Dead until I got it going again. Now it is the most vibrant place of its kind on the Planet...And we have Space Force to go along with it. We have accomplished more than any Administration in first 3 1/2 years. Sorry, but it all doesn't happen with Sleepy Joe!

THE WOODWARD BOOKS

Veteran journalist Bob Woodward published his first of three books about President Trump, "Fear: Trump in the White House," at the end of the president's second year in office. The president, predictably, headed straight to Twitter to discredit the book's numerous allegations of chaos and to accuse the author of trying to influence the results of the upcoming 2018 midterm elections.

Donald J. Trump ✔ @realDonaldTrump · Sep 4, 2018

The Woodward book has already been refuted and discredited by General (Secretary of Defense) James Mattis and General (Chief of Staff) John Kelly. Their quotes were made up frauds, a con on the public. Likewise other stories and quotes. Woodward is a Dem operative? Notice timing?

Donald J. Trump ✔ @realDonaldTrump · Sep 4, 2018

The already discredited Woodward book, so many lies and phony sources, has me calling Jeff Sessions "mentally retarded" and "a dumb southerner." I said NEITHER, never used those terms on anyone, including Jeff, and being a southerner is a GREAT thing. He made this up to divide!

Donald J. Trump ✔ @realDonaldTrump · Sep 7, 2018

The Woodward book is a scam. I don't talk the way I am quoted. If I did I would not have been elected President. These quotes were made up. The author uses every trick in the book to demean and belittle. I wish the people could see the real facts - and our country is doing GREAT!

Donald J. Trump ✔ @realDonaldTrump · Sep 10, 2018

The Woodward book is a Joke - just another assault against me, in a barrage of assaults, using now disproven unnamed and anonymous sources. Many have already come forward to say the quotes by them, like the book, are fiction. Dems can't stand losing. I'll write the real book!

Donald J. Trump ✔ @realDonaldTrump · Aug 14, 2020

The Bob Woodward book will be a FAKE, as always, just as many of the others have been. But, believe it or not, lately I've been getting lots of GREAT books!

HURRICANES

President Trump never caught a break with hurricanes. First, photos of him tossing rolls of paper towels to victims of Hurricane Maria in Puerto Rico were mocked. Then he was quoted suggesting the military should stop hurricanes with nuclear bombs. Later, he caused a stir when he announced that Alabama was in Hurricane Dorian's path when, at that moment, it was not.

Donald J. Trump ✔ @realDonaldTrump · Sep 12, 2018

We got A Pluses for our recent hurricane work in Texas and Florida (and did an unappreciated great job in Puerto Rico, even though an inaccessible island with very poor electricity and a totally incompetent Mayor of San Juan). We are ready for the big one that is coming!

Donald J. Trump ✔ @realDonaldTrump · Aug 26, 2019

Just returned to Washington from France and the very successful G-7, only to find that the Fake News is still trying to perpetuate the phony story that I wanted to use Nuclear weapons to blow up hurricanes before they reach shore. This is so ridiculous, never happened!

Donald J. Trump ✔ @realDonaldTrump · Aug 27, 2019

Axios (whatever that is) sat back and said GEEEEE, let's see, what can we make up today to embarrass the President? Then they said, "why don't we say he wants to bomb a hurricane, that should do it!" The media in our Country is totally out of control!

Donald J. Trump ✔ @realDonaldTrump · Sep 5, 2019

Alabama was going to be hit or grazed, and then Hurricane Dorian took a different path (up along the East Coast). The Fake News knows this very well. That's why they're the Fake News!

Donald J. Trump ✔ @realDonaldTrump · Sep 6, 2019

The Fake News Media was fixated on the fact that I properly said, at the beginnings of Hurricane Dorian, that in addition to Florida & other states, Alabama may also be grazed or hit. They went Crazy, hoping against hope that I made a mistake (which I didn't). Check out maps.

MY FRIEND KIM JONG UN

By 2019, long-gone were the days of President Trump calling North Korea's Kim Jong Un "short and fat." Instead, the president flaunted his newfound friendship with the communist leader. As a sign of how their relationship had blossomed over the years, the president told a rally crowd in late 2021 that he gifted Kim Jong Un a cassette of Elton John's 1972 hit song "Rocket Man."

Donald J. Trump ✓ @realDonaldTrump · Feb 26, 2019

Vietnam is thriving like few places on earth. North Korea would be the same, and very quickly, if it would denuclearize. The potential is AWESOME, a great opportunity, like almost none other in history, for my friend Kim Jong Un. We will know fairly soon - Very Interesting!

Donald J. Trump ✓ @realDonaldTrump · Apr 13, 2019

I agree with Kim Jong Un of North Korea that our personal relationship remains very good, perhaps the term excellent would be even more accurate, and that a third Summit would be good in that we fully understand where we each stand. North Korea has tremendous potential for extraordinary growth.

Donald J. Trump ✓ @realDonaldTrump · May 28, 2019

I was actually sticking up for Sleepy Joe Biden while on foreign soil. Kim Jong Un called him a "low IQ idiot," and many other things, whereas I related the quote of Chairman Kim as a much softer "low IQ individual." Who could possibly be upset with that?

Donald J. Trump ✓ @realDonaldTrump · Dec 15, 2020

It was great being with Chairman Kim Jong Un of North Korea this weekend. We had a great meeting, he looked really well and very healthy - I look forward to seeing him again soon.

Donald J. Trump ✓ @realDonaldTrump · Sep 10, 2020

Kim Jong Un is in good health. Never underestimate him!

THE CALIFORNIA WILDFIRES

During his time in the White House, President Trump was highly critical of politicians in California, a state whose significant chunk of electoral votes hasn't tilted toward a Republican presidential candidate since 1988. He often tweeted about the state's wildfires, energy blackouts, and water shortages as evidence of Democratic mismanagement of the state's government and budget.

Donald J. Trump @realDonaldTrump · Nov 10, 2018

There is no reason for these massive, deadly and costly forest fires in California except that forest management is so poor. Billions of dollars are given each year, with so many lives lost, all because of gross mismanagement of the forests. Remedy now, or no more Fed payments!

Donald J. Trump @realDonaldTrump · Jan 19, 2019

Billions of dollars are sent to the State of California for Forest fires that, with proper Forest Management, would never happen. Unless they get their act together, which is unlikely, I have ordered FEMA to send no more money. It is a disgraceful situation in lives & money!

Donald J. Trump @realDonaldTrump · Nov 3, 2019

The Governor of California, @GavinNewsom, has done a terrible job of forest management. I told him from the first day we met that he must "clean" his forest floors regardless of what his bosses, the environmentalists, DEMAND of him. Must also do burns and cut fire stoppers.

Donald J. Trump @realDonaldTrump · Nov 3, 2019

The Democrats are Fixers, and they are working overtime to FIX the Impeachment "Process" in order to hurt the Republican Party and me. Nancy Pelosi should instead Fix her broken District and Corrupt Adam should clean up & manage the California forests which are always burning!

Donald J. Trump @realDonaldTrump · Oct 11, 2020

Turn California around. No more shutdowns, rolling blackouts, forest fires (management), or water rationing (because millions of gallons are stupidly routed out into the Pacific Ocean). VOTE TRUMP!

THE FEDERAL RESERVE

President Trump raged against the Federal Reserve, the central banking system of the United States, as far back as the announcement of his presidential campaign. The president argued that the chair of the Federal Reserve, Jay Powell, was holding America back from its economic potential, even going so far as to compare him to communist President Xi Jinping of China.

Donald J. Trump ✔ @realDonaldTrump · Jul 5, 2019

As well as we are doing from the day after the great Election, when the Market shot right up, it could have been even better - massive additional wealth would have been created, & used very well. Our most difficult problem is not our competitors, it is the Federal Reserve!

Donald J. Trump ✔ @realDonaldTrump · Aug 28, 2019

Our Federal Reserve cannot "mentally" keep up with the competition - other countries. At the G-7 in France, all of the other Leaders were giddy about how low their Interest Costs have gone. Germany is actually "getting paid" to borrow money - ZERO INTEREST PLUS! No Clue Fed!

Donald J. Trump ✔ @realDonaldTrump · Aug 23, 2019

My only question is, who is our bigger enemy, Jay Powell or Chairman Xi?

Donald J. Trump ✔ @realDonaldTrump · Sep 11, 2019

The USA should always be paying the the lowest rate. No Inflation! It is only the naïveté of Jay Powell and the Federal Reserve that doesn't allow us to do what other countries are already doing. A once in a lifetime opportunity that we are missing because of "Boneheads."

Donald J. Trump ✔ @realDonaldTrump · Sep 18, 2019

Jay Powell and the Federal Reserve Fail Again. No "guts," no sense, no vision! A terrible communicator!

A PERFECT PHONE CALL

In September 2019, during a routine call with the president of Ukraine, President Trump was quoted saying, "I would like you to do us a favor" before asking the president to look into a long-discredited conspiracy theory that challenges Russia's involvement in the 2016 hacking of DNC servers. The phone call ultimately led to the first of President Trump's two impeachments.

Donald J. Trump ✓ @realDonaldTrump · Sep 27, 2019

If that perfect phone call with the President of Ukraine Isn't considered appropriate, then no future President can EVER again speak to another foreign leader!

Donald J. Trump ✓ @realDonaldTrump · Oct 29, 2019

How many more Never Trumpers will be allowed to testify about a perfectly appropriate phone call when all anyone has to do is READ THE TRANSCRIPT! I knew people were listening in on the call (why would I say something inappropriate?), which was fine with me, but why so many?

Donald J. Trump ✓ @realDonaldTrump · Nov 4, 2019

What I said on the phone call with the Ukrainian President is "perfectly" stated. There is no reason to call witnesses to analyze my words and meaning. This is just another Democrat Hoax that I have had to live with from the day I got elected (and before!). Disgraceful!

Donald J. Trump ✓ @realDonaldTrump · Dec 15, 2019

A PERFECT phone call. "Can you do us (not me. Us is referring to our Country) a favor." Then go on to talk about "Country" and "U.S. Attorney General." The Impeachment Hoax is just a continuation of the Witch Hunt which has been going on for 3 years. We will win! #MAGAKAG #2020

Donald J. Trump ✓ @realDonaldTrump · Jan 16, 2020

I JUST GOT IMPEACHED FOR MAKING A PERFECT PHONE CALL!

THE WHISTLEBLOWERS

The Trump administration was rife with whistleblower complaints. From the Department of Homeland Security to the Department of Health & Human Services, government employees filed reports alleging questionable commands, controversial actions, and potentially criminal words. President Trump used his Twitter account to denounce the whistleblowers that made headlines.

Donald J. Trump ✔ @realDonaldTrump · Sep 27, 2019

Sounding more and more like the so-called Whistleblower isn't a Whistleblower at all. In addition, all second hand information that proved to be so inaccurate that there may not have even been somebody else, a leaker or spy, feeding it to him or her? A partisan operative?

Donald J. Trump ✔ @realDonaldTrump · Oct 9, 2019

The so-called Whistleblower, before knowing I was going to release the exact Transcript, stated that my call with the Ukrainian President was "crazy, frightening, and completely lacking in substance related to national security." This is a very big Lie. Read the Transcript!

Donald J. Trump ✔ @realDonaldTrump · Nov 4, 2019

The Whistleblower gave false information & dealt with corrupt politician Schiff. He must be brought forward to testify. Written answers not acceptable! Where is the 2nd Whistleblower? He disappeared after I released the transcript. Does he even exist? Where is the informant? Con!

Donald J. Trump ✔ @realDonaldTrump · Feb 3, 2020

Where's the Whistleblower? Where's the second Whistleblower? Where's the Informer? Why did Corrupt politician Schiff MAKE UP my conversation with the Ukrainian President??? Why didn't the House do its job? And sooo much more!

Donald J. Trump ✔ @realDonaldTrump · May 14, 2020

I don't know the so-called Whistleblower Rick Bright, never met him or even heard of him, but to me he is a disgruntled employee, not liked or respected by people I spoke to and who, with his attitude, should no longer be working for our government!

PROFESSIONAL SPORTS

When professional athletes like football player Colin Kaepernick began to kneel during the national anthem in protest of police brutality, President Trump chimed in on the controversy on Twitter. He argued that the NFL (and NBA and others) should require athletes to stand for the national anthem and blamed the sport's low television ratings on their refusal to do so.

Donald J. Trump ✔ @realDonaldTrump · Aug 10, 2018

The NFL players are at it again - taking a knee when they should be standing proudly for the National Anthem. Numerous players, from different teams, wanted to show their "outrage" at something that most of them are unable to define. They make a fortune doing what they love.

Donald J. Trump ✔ @realDonaldTrump · Sep 5, 2018

Just like the NFL, whose ratings have gone WAY DOWN, Nike is getting absolutely killed with anger and boycotts. I wonder if they had any idea that it would be this way? As far as the NFL is concerned, I just find it hard to watch, and always will, until they stand for the FLAG!

Donald J. Trump ✔ @realDonaldTrump · Jul 6, 2020

Has @BubbaWallace apologized to all of those great NASCAR drivers & officials who came to his aid, stood by his side, & were willing to sacrifice everything for him, only to find out that the whole thing was just another HOAX? That & Flag decision has caused lowest ratings EVER!

Donald J. Trump ✔ @realDonaldTrump · Jul 6, 2020

They name teams out of STRENGTH, not weakness, but now the Washington Redskins & Cleveland Indians, two fabled sports franchises, look like they are going to be changing their names in order to be politically correct. Indians, like Elizabeth Warren, must be very angry right now!

Donald J. Trump ✔ @realDonaldTrump · Sep 1, 2020

People are tired of watching the highly political @NBA. Basketball ratings are WAY down, and they won't be coming back. I hope football and baseball are watching and learning because the same thing will be happening to them. Stand tall for our Country and our Flag!!!

FORMER WHITE HOUSE OFFICIALS

The unusually high turnover rate of White House officials during President Trump's four years in the Oval Office stemmed from both firings and resignations. While some exiting members of the president's administration were given gracious send-offs on Twitter, others were ridiculed with alliterative nicknames and other insults and occasionally accused of committing treason.

Donald J. Trump ✔ @realDonaldTrump · Dec 2, 2017

I had to fire General Flynn because he lied to the Vice President and the FBI. He has pled guilty to those lies. It is a shame because his actions during the transition were lawful. There was nothing to hide!

Donald J. Trump ✔ @realDonaldTrump · Jan 5, 2018

Michael Wolff is a total loser who made up stories in order to sell this really boring and untruthful book. He used Sloppy Steve Bannon, who cried when he got fired and begged for his job. Now Sloppy Steve has been dumped like a dog by almost everyone. Too bad!

Donald J. Trump ✔ @realDonaldTrump · Jun 25, 2018

The Red Hen Restaurant should focus more on cleaning its filthy canopies, doors and windows (badly needs a paint job) rather than refusing to serve a fine person like Sarah Huckabee Sanders. I always had a rule, if a restaurant is dirty on the outside, it is dirty on the inside!

Donald J. Trump ✔ @realDonaldTrump · Aug 29, 2018

White House Counsel Don McGahn will be leaving his position in the fall, shortly after the confirmation (hopefully) of Judge Brett Kavanaugh to the United States Supreme Court. I have worked with Don for a long time and truly appreciate his service!

Donald J. Trump ✔ @realDonaldTrump · Jan 12, 2019

Lyin' James Comey, Andrew McCabe, Peter S and his lover, agent Lisa Page, & more, all disgraced and/or fired and caught in the act. These are just some of the losers that tried to do a number on your President. Part of the Witch Hunt. Remember the "insurance policy?" This is it!

MORE FORMER WH OFFICIALS

President Trump's former White House officials made a variety of career moves after leaving their positions. Many authored books — some supportive of the president, others highly critical — about their time in the Trump administration. Some became professional commentators on Fox News, others ran for political office themselves, and one took part in a reality tv show.

Donald J. Trump ✔ @realDonaldTrump · Aug 31, 2019

Yes, I am currently suing various people for violating their confidentiality agreements. Disgusting and foul mouthed Omarosa is one. I gave her every break, despite the fact that she was despised by everyone, and she went for some cheap money from a book. Numerous others also!

Donald J. Trump ✔ @realDonaldTrump · Nov 11, 2019

Vote for Sean Spicer on Dancing with the Stars. He is a great and very loyal guy who is working very hard. He is in the quarterfinals - all the way with Sean! #MAGA #KAG

Donald J. Trump ✔ @realDonaldTrump · Feb 13, 2020

When I terminated John Kelly, which I couldn't do fast enough, he knew full well that he was way over his head. Being Chief of Staff just wasn't for him. He came in with a bang, went out with a whimper, but like so many X's, he misses the action & just can't keep his mouth shut,.

Donald J. Trump ✔ @realDonaldTrump · Jun 9, 2020

Mattis was our Country's most overrated General. He talked a lot, but never "brought home the bacon." He was terrible! Someday I will tell the real story on him and others - both good and bad!

Donald J. Trump ✔ @realDonaldTrump · Nov 25, 2020

It is my Great Honor to announce that General Michael T. Flynn has been granted a Full Pardon. Congratulations to @GenFlynn and his wonderful family, I know you will now have a truly fantastic Thanksgiving!

Though President Trump initially praised President Xi Jinping's response to the rapid spread of COVID-19 throughout China, tweeting "Much respect!" at the communist leader in March 2020, he quickly banned travel into the United States from China, eventually doubled down on the controversial coronavirus nickname "the China Virus," and blamed China for the pandemic itself.

Donald J. Trump @realDonaldTrump · May 25, 2020

Great reviews on our handling of Covid 19, sometimes referred to as the China Virus. Ventilators, Testing, Medical Supply Distribution, we made a lot of Governors look very good - And got no credit for so doing. Most importantly, we helped a lot of great people!

Donald J. Trump @realDonaldTrump · Jul 20, 2020

We are United in our effort to defeat the Invisible China Virus, and many people say that it is Patriotic to wear a face mask when you can't socially distance. There is nobody more Patriotic than me, your favorite President!

Donald J. Trump @realDonaldTrump · Aug 3, 2020

So Crazy Nancy Pelosi said horrible things about Dr. Deborah Birx, going after her because she was too positive on the very good job we are doing on combatting the China Virus, including Vaccines & Therapeutics. In order to counter Nancy, Deborah took the bait & hit us. Pathetic!

Donald J. Trump @realDonaldTrump · Aug 7, 2020

I called the politicization of the China Virus by the Radical Left Democrats a Hoax, not the China Virus itself. Everybody knows this except for the Fake and very Corrupt Media!

Donald J. Trump @realDonaldTrump · Sep 8, 2020

Because of the China Virus, my Campaign, which has raised a lot of money, was forced to spend in order to counter the Fake News reporting about the way we handled it (China Ban, etc.). We did, and are doing, a GREAT job, and have a lot of money left over, much more than 2016.

THE U.S. POSTAL SERVICE

During his term, President Trump was highly critical of the U.S. Postal Service's annual deficits and its business relationship with Amazon. The USPS, which began to lose billions of dollars in 2006 after the passage of a unique law requiring the federal agency to pre-fund its retirees' benefits, is 99% funded by the sale of stamps and postage and just 1% by taxpayer money.

Donald J. Trump ✔ @realDonaldTrump · Dec 29, 2017

Why is the United States Post Office, which is losing many billions of dollars a year, while charging Amazon and others so little to deliver their packages, making Amazon richer and the Post Office dumber and poorer? Should be charging MUCH MORE!

Donald J. Trump ✔ @realDonaldTrump · Apr 3, 2018

I am right about Amazon costing the United States Post Office massive amounts of money for being their Delivery Boy. Amazon should pay these costs (plus) and not have them bourne by the American Taxpayer. Many billions of dollars. P.O. leaders don't have a clue (or do they?)!

Donald J. Trump ✔ @realDonaldTrump · Apr 24, 2020

I will never let our Post Office fail. It has been mismanaged for years, especially since the advent of the internet and modern-day technology. The people that work there are great, and we're going to keep them happy, healthy, and well!

Donald J. Trump ✔ @realDonaldTrump · Aug 17, 2020

The U.S. Post Office (System) has been failing for many decades. We simply want to MAKE THE POST OFFICE GREAT AGAIN, while at the same time saving billions of dollars a year for American Taxpayers. Dems don't have a clue! @USPostOffice911

Donald J. Trump ✔ @realDonaldTrump · Aug 18, 2020

.@Amazon, and others in that business, should be charged (by the U.S. Postal System) much more per package, and the Post Office would be immediately brought back to "good health", now vibrant, with ALL jobs saved. No pass on to customers. Get it done!

REPUBLICAN LEADERSHIP

President Trump's relationship with Republican leadership during his time in the White House was as unpredictable as a high school romance. Sometimes the president would praise leaders of the Republican party for their votes, tweets, and public statements of support. Other times, often when GOP politicians publicly disagreed with or criticized him, he'd call them out on Twitter.

Donald J. Trump @realDonaldTrump · Jul 5, 2018

Thanks to REPUBLICAN LEADERSHIP, America is WINNING AGAIN - and America is being RESPECTED again all over the world. Because we are finally putting AMERICA FIRST!

Donald J. Trump @realDonaldTrump · Sep 15, 2018

When will Republican leadership learn that they are being played like a fiddle by the Democrats on Border Security and Building the Wall? Without Borders, we don't have a country. With Open Borders, which the Democrats want, we have nothing but crime! Finish the Wall!

Donald J. Trump @realDonaldTrump · Nov 22, 2019

Thank you to @senatemajldr Mitch McConnell and @GOPLeader Kevin McCarthy for their Great Leadership! There has never been so much unity and spirit in the Republican Party, as there is right now!

Donald J. Trump @realDonaldTrump · Dec 29, 2020

Weak and tired Republican "leadership" will allow the bad Defense Bill to pass. Say goodbye to VITAL Section 230 termination, your National Monuments, Forts (names!) and Treasures (inserted by Elizabeth "Pocahontas" Warren), 5G, and our great soldiers being removed and brought home from foreign lands.

Donald J. Trump @realDonaldTrump · Dec 29, 2020

Can you imagine if the Republicans stole a Presidential Election from the Democrats - All hell would break out. Republican leadership only wants the path of least resistance. Our leaders (not me, of course!) are pathetic. They only know how to lose! P.S. I got MANY Senators and Congressmen/Congresswomen Elected.

THE 2020 ELECTION

Following his loss in the 2020 presidential election, President Trump expressed his opinion of the results on Twitter, tweeting without evidence that millions of mail-in votes were fraudulent, that the election was stolen, that President-elect Joe Biden was a "fake president," and that his supporters should gather for a big protest in Washington, D.C. on January 6, 2021.

Donald J. Trump ✔ @realDonaldTrump · Dec 19, 2020

Peter Navarro releases 36-page report alleging election fraud 'more than sufficient' to swing victory to Trump. A great report by Peter. Statistically impossible to have lost the 2020 Election. Big protest in D.C. on January 6th. Be there, will be wild!

Donald J. Trump ✔ @realDonaldTrump · Dec 26, 2020

The "Justice" Department and the FBI have done nothing about the 2020 Presidential Election Voter Fraud, the biggest SCAM in our nation's history, despite overwhelming evidence. They should be ashamed. History will remember. Never give up. See everyone in D.C. on January 6th.

Donald J. Trump ✔ @realDonaldTrump · Dec 26, 2020

The U.S. Supreme Court has been totally incompetent and weak on the massive Election Fraud that took place in the 2020 Presidential Election. We have absolute PROOF, but they don't want to see it - No "standing", they say. If we have corrupt elections, we have no country!

Donald J. Trump ✔ @realDonaldTrump · Dec 26, 2020

A young military man working in Afghanistan told me that elections in Afghanistan are far more secure and much better run than the USA's 2020 Election. Ours, with its millions and millions of corrupt Mail-In Ballots, was the election of a third world country. Fake President!

Donald J. Trump ✔ @realDonaldTrump · Dec 26, 2020

The "Justice" Department and the FBI have done nothing about the 2020 Presidential Election Voter Fraud, the biggest SCAM in our nation's history, despite overwhelming evidence. They should be ashamed. History will remember. Never give up. See everyone in D.C. on January 6th.

THE FINAL TWEETS

Twitter permanently banned President Trump from his favorite social media platform on January 8, 2021. The company tweeted, "After close review of recent Tweets from the @realDonaldTrump account and the context around them we have permanently suspended the account due to the risk of further incitement of violence." These are the president's final tweets.

Donald J. Trump ✓ @realDonaldTrump · Jan 6, 2021

Mike Pence didn't have the courage to do what should have been done to protect our Country and our Constitution, giving States a chance to certify a corrected set of facts, not the fraudulent or inaccurate ones which they were asked to previously certify. USA demands the truth!

Donald J. Trump ✓ @realDonaldTrump · Jan 6, 2021

Please support our Capitol Police and Law Enforcement. They are truly on the side of our Country. Stay peaceful! I am asking for everyone at the U.S. Capitol to remain peaceful. No violence! Remember, WE are the Party of Law & Order – respect the Law and our great men and women in Blue. Thank you!

Donald J. Trump ✓ @realDonaldTrump · Jan 6, 2021

These are the things and events that happen when a sacred landslide election victory is so unceremoniously & viciously stripped away from great patriots who have been badly & unfairly treated for so long. Go home with love & in peace. Remember this day forever!

Donald J. Trump ✓ @realDonaldTrump · Jan 8, 2021

The 75,000,000 great American Patriots who voted for me, AMERICA FIRST, and MAKE AMERICA GREAT AGAIN, will have a GIANT VOICE long into the future. They will not be disrespected or treated unfairly in any way, shape or form!!!

Donald J. Trump ✓ @realDonaldTrump · Jan 8, 2021

To all of those who have asked, I will not be going to the Inauguration on January 20th.

THE DO NOTHING PARTY

When the Republican-controlled House and Senate failed to pass legislation that addressed the issues he promised to take care of on the campaign trail, President Trump blamed the Democrats for obstructing his agenda and dubbed them the "Do Nothing Party." The president tweeted about Democrats 4,390 times during his term, making them by far his most prolific Twitter topic.

 Donald J. Trump ✔ @realDonaldTrump · May 23, 2019

The Democrats have become known as THE DO NOTHING PARTY!

 Donald J. Trump ✔ @realDonaldTrump · Oct 2, 2019

The Do Nothing Democrats should be focused on building up our Country, not wasting everyone's time and energy on BULLSHIT, which is what they have been doing ever since I got overwhelmingly elected in 2016, 223-306. Get a better candidate this time, you'll need it!

 Donald J. Trump ✔ @realDonaldTrump · Nov 24, 2019

Nancy Pelosi, Adam Schiff, AOC and the rest of the Democrats are not getting important legislation done, hence, the Do Nothing Democrats. USMCA, National Defense Authorization Act, Gun Safety, Prescription Drug Prices, & Infrastructure are dead in the water because of the Dems!

 Donald J. Trump ✔ @realDonaldTrump · Dec 5, 2019

The Do Nothing, Radical Left Democrats have just announced that they are going to seek to Impeach me over NOTHING. They already gave up on the ridiculous Mueller "stuff," so now they hang their hats on two totally appropriate (perfect) phone calls with the Ukrainian President.

 Donald J. Trump ✔ @realDonaldTrump · Dec 18, 2019

SUCH ATROCIOUS LIES BY THE RADICAL LEFT, DO NOTHING DEMOCRATS. THIS IS AN ASSAULT ON AMERICA, AND AN ASSAULT ON THE REPUBLICAN PARTY!!!!

CROOKED HILLARY CLINTON

Throughout his presidential campaign, Donald J. Trump lobbed accusations of corruption at his Democratic opponent. He incessantly questioned her use of a private email server during her time as Secretary of State, wondered aloud why she, former President Obama, and other Democrats were not in prison, and encouraged chants of "lock her up" at his campaign rallies.

 Donald J. Trump ✔ @realDonaldTrump · May 31, 2017

Crooked Hillary Clinton now blames everybody but herself, refuses to say she was a terrible candidate. Hits Facebook & even Dems & DNC.

 Donald J. Trump ✔ @realDonaldTrump · Jul 22, 2017

My son Donald openly gave his e-mails to the media & authorities whereas Crooked Hillary Clinton deleted (& acid washed) her 33,000 e-mails!

 Donald J. Trump ✔ @realDonaldTrump · Nov 11, 2017

Does the Fake News Media remember when Crooked Hillary Clinton, as Secretary of State, was begging Russia to be our friend with the misspelled reset button? Obama tried also, but he had zero chemistry with Putin.

 Donald J. Trump ✔ @realDonaldTrump · Nov 18, 2017

Crooked Hillary Clinton is the worst (and biggest) loser of all time. She just can't stop, which is so good for the Republican Party. Hillary, get on with your life and give it another try in three years!

 Donald J. Trump ✔ @realDonaldTrump · Mar 22, 2018

Remember when they were saying, during the campaign, that Donald Trump is giving great speeches and drawing big crowds, but he is spending much less money and not using social media as well as Crooked Hillary's large and highly sophisticated staff. Well, not saying that anymore!

FORMER PRESIDENT OBAMA

An early and vocal supporter of the discredited birther conspiracy, President Trump, predictably, often used his social media platform to criticize former President Obama. He denounced the Democratic former president's foreign policy decisions, criticized the Affordable Care Act, and accused his administration of failing to address Russian meddling ahead of the 2016 election.

Donald J. Trump ✔ @realDonaldTrump · Jun 13, 2018

Before taking office people were assuming that we were going to War with North Korea. President Obama said that North Korea was our biggest and most dangerous problem. No longer - sleep well tonight!

Donald J. Trump ✔ @realDonaldTrump · Dec 30, 2018

President and Mrs. Obama built/has a ten foot Wall around their D.C. mansion/compound. I agree, totally necessary for their safety and security. The U.S. needs the same thing, slightly larger version!

Donald J. Trump ✔ @realDonaldTrump · Jun 9, 2019

If President Obama made the deals that I have made, both at the Border and for the Economy, the Corrupt Media would be hailing them as Incredible, & a National Holiday would be immediately declared. With me, despite our record setting Economy and all that I have done, no credit!

Donald J. Trump ✔ @realDonaldTrump · Feb 17, 2020

Did you hear the latest con job? President Obama is now trying to take credit for the Economic Boom taking place under the Trump Administration. He had the WEAKEST recovery since the Great Depression, despite Zero Fed Rate & MASSIVE quantitative easing. NOW, best jobs numbers.

Donald J. Trump ✔ @realDonaldTrump · Jul 23, 2020

Obama, who wouldn't even endorse Biden until everyone else was out of the primaries (and even then waited a long time!), is now making a commercial of support. Remember, I wouldn't even be here if it weren't for them. I wouldn't be President. They did a terrible job!

SHIFTY LIDDLE' ADAM SCHIFF

Congressman Adam Schiff led the charge against President Trump during the Special Counsel investigation into Russian interference in the 2016 election, repeatedly claiming there was evidence that the Trump team had colluded with the Russian government to influence the results. The president tweeted that, along with other Democrats, Schiff should be arrested for treason.

Donald J. Trump ✓ @realDonaldTrump · Feb 18, 2018

Finally, Liddle' Adam Schiff, the leakin' monster of no control, is now blaming the Obama Administration for Russian meddling in the 2016 Election. He is finally right about something. Obama was President, knew of the threat, and did nothing. Thank you Adam!

Donald J. Trump ✓ @realDonaldTrump · Sep 26, 2019

Liddle' Adam Schiff, who has worked unsuccessfully for 3 years to hurt the Republican Party and President, has just said that the Whistleblower, even though he or she only had second hand information, "is credible." How can that be with zero info and a known bias. Democrat Scam!

Donald J. Trump ✓ @realDonaldTrump · Sep 27, 2019

To show you how dishonest the LameStream Media is, I used the word Liddle', not Liddle, in discribing Corrupt Congressman Liddle' Adam Schiff. Low ratings @CNN purposely took the hyphen out and said I spelled the word little wrong. A small but never ending situation with CNN!

Donald J. Trump ✓ @realDonaldTrump · Jan 25, 2020

Our case against lyin', cheatin', liddle' Adam "Shifty" Schiff, Cryin' Chuck Schumer, Nervous Nancy Pelosi, their leader, dumb as a rock AOC, & the entire Radical Left, Do Nothing Democrat Party, starts today at 10:00 A.M. on @FoxNews, @OANN or Fake News @CNN or Fake News MSDNC!

Donald J. Trump ✓ @realDonaldTrump · Feb 23, 2020

Somebody please tell incompetent (thanks for my high poll numbers) & corrupt politician Adam "Shifty" Schiff to stop leaking Classified information or, even worse, made up information, to the Fake News Media. Someday he will be caught, & that will be a very unpleasant experience!

NERVOUS NANCY PELOSI

Then-House Minority Leader Nancy Pelosi vocally opposed President Trump's agenda — and the president vocally opposed her on Twitter. He tweeted that Pelosi should be impeached and arrested for treason, claimed that nearly every Democrat running for office during the 2018 midterms was a Pelosi puppet, and ultimately blamed her for his two impeachments.

Donald J. Trump ✓ @realDonaldTrump · Jun 7, 2019

Nervous Nancy Pelosi is a disgrace to herself and her family for having made such a disgusting statement, especially since I was with foreign leaders overseas. There is no evidence for such a thing to have been said. Nervous Nancy & Dems are getting Zero work done in Congress.

Donald J. Trump ✓ @realDonaldTrump · Oct 6, 2019

This makes Nervous Nancy every bit as guilty as Liddle' Adam Schiff for High Crimes and Misdemeanors, and even Treason. I guess that means that they, along with all of those that evilly "Colluded" with them, must all be immediately Impeached!

Donald J. Trump ✓ @realDonaldTrump · Oct 29, 2019

Nervous Nancy Pelosi is doing everything possible to destroy the Republican Party. Our Polls show that it is going to be just the opposite. The Do Nothing Dems will lose many seats in 2020. They have a Death Wish, led by a corrupt politician, Adam Schiff!

Donald J. Trump ✓ @realDonaldTrump · Feb 7, 2020

Another win just in. Nervous Nancy Pelosi and the Democrats in Congress sued me, thrown out. This one unanimous, in the D.C. Circuit. Witch Hunt!

Donald J. Trump ✓ @realDonaldTrump · Apr 19, 2020

Nervous Nancy is an inherently "dumb" person. She wasted all of her time on the Impeachment Hoax. She will be overthrown, either by inside or out, just like her last time as "Speaker". Wallace & @FoxNews are on a bad path, watch!

CRYIN' CHUCK SCHUMER

President Trump referred to then-Senate Minority Leader Chuck Schumer as Nancy Pelosi's "sidekick" and accused him of leading the Senate Democrats in obstructing his agenda. The president's favorite nickname for the California congressman originated when he watched Schumer give a teary-eyed speech against the travel ban during his first month as president.

Donald J. Trump ✔ @realDonaldTrump · Jan 31, 2017

Nancy Pelosi and Fake Tears Chuck Schumer held a rally at the steps of The Supreme Court and mic did not work (a mess)-just like Dem party!

Donald J. Trump ✔ @realDonaldTrump · Jun 30, 2018

Either we need to elect more Republicans in November or Republicans must end the ridiculous 60 vote, or Filibuster, rule - or better yet, do both. Cryin' Chuck would do it on day one, but we'll never give him the chance. Some great legislation awaits - be smart!

Donald J. Trump ✔ @realDonaldTrump · Jan 10, 2019

Cryin Chuck told his favorite lie when he used his standard sound bite that I "slammed the table & walked out of the room. He had a temper tantrum." Because I knew he would say that, and after Nancy said no to proper Border Security, I politely said bye-bye and left, no slamming!

Donald J. Trump ✔ @realDonaldTrump · Jun 4, 2019

Can you imagine Cryin' Chuck Schumer saying out loud, for all to hear, that I am bluffing with respect to putting Tariffs on Mexico. What a Creep. He would rather have our Country fail with drugs & Immigration than give Republicans a win. But he gave Mexico bad advice, no bluff!

Donald J. Trump ✔ @realDonaldTrump · Dec 14, 2019

Chuck Schumer sat for years during the Obama Administration and watched as China ripped off the United States. He & the Do Nothing Democrats did NOTHING as this $ carnage took place. Now, without even seeing it, he snipes at our GREAT new deal with China. Too bad Cryin' Chuck!

THE SQUAD

Never one to let a critic go unpunished on Twitter, President Trump called out "The Squad," a group of then-freshman Democratic congresswomen who were vocal about their disapproval of the president. He made headlines with one particular series of tweets, all included below, in which he told The Squad to return to their home countries. All but one was born in America.

Donald J. Trump ✅ @realDonaldTrump · Jul 14, 2019

So interesting to see "Progressive" Democrat Congresswomen, who originally came from countries whose governments are a complete and total catastrophe, the worst, most corrupt and inept anywhere in the world (if they even have a functioning government at all), now loudly......

Donald J. Trump ✅ @realDonaldTrump · Jul 14, 2019

....and viciously telling the people of the United States, the greatest and most powerful Nation on earth, how our government is to be run. Why don't they go back and help fix the totally broken and crime infested places from which they came. Then come back and show us how....

Donald J. Trump ✅ @realDonaldTrump · Jul 14, 2019

....it is done. These places need your help badly, you can't leave fast enough. I'm sure that Nancy Pelosi would be very happy to quickly work out free travel arrangements!

Donald J. Trump ✅ @realDonaldTrump · Jul 22, 2019

The "Squad" is a very Racist group of troublemakers who are young, inexperienced, and not very smart. They are pulling the once great Democrat Party far left, and were against humanitarian aid at the Border...And are now against ICE and Homeland Security. So bad for our Country!

Donald J. Trump ✅ @realDonaldTrump · Sep 2, 2019

The Amazon Washington Post did a story that I brought racist attacks against the "Squad." No, they brought racist attacks against our Nation. All I do is call them out for the horrible things they have said. The Democrats have become the Party of the Squad!

POCAHONTAS

President Trump used the indigenous slur "Pocahontas" to taunt Senator Elizabeth Warren after she claimed to have Native American heritage. He even went so far as to pledge $1 million to the charity of Warren's choice if she agreed to take a DNA test that proved she had Native American ancestors. A few months later, she did. President Trump never donated the money.

Donald J. Trump @realDonaldTrump · Oct 16, 2018

Pocahontas (the bad version), sometimes referred to as Elizabeth Warren, is getting slammed. She took a bogus DNA test and it showed that she may be 1/1024, far less than the average American. Now Cherokee Nation denies her, "DNA test is useless." Even they don't want her. Phony!

Donald J. Trump @realDonaldTrump · Jan 13, 2019

If Elizabeth Warren, often referred to by me as Pocahontas, did this commercial from Bighorn or Wounded Knee instead of her kitchen, with her husband dressed in full Indian garb, it would have been a smash!

Donald J. Trump @realDonaldTrump · Feb 9, 2019

Today Elizabeth Warren, sometimes referred to by me as Pocahontas, joined the race for President. Will she run as our first Native American presidential candidate, or has she decided that after 32 years, this is not playing so well anymore? See you on the campaign TRAIL, Liz!

Donald J. Trump @realDonaldTrump · Mar 4, 2020

Wow! If Elizabeth Warren wasn't in the race, Bernie Sanders would have EASILY won Massachusetts, Minnesota and Texas, not to mention various other states. Our modern day Pocahontas won't go down in history as a winner, but she may very well go down as the all time great SPOILER!

Donald J. Trump @realDonaldTrump · Jun 11, 2020

Seriously failed presidential candidate, Senator Elizabeth "Pocahontas" Warren, just introduced an Amendment on the renaming of many of our legendary Military Bases from which we trained to WIN two World Wars. Hopefully our great Republican Senators won't fall for this!

CRAZY BERNIE SANDERS

On the campaign trail, President Trump stoked the flames of rivalry between then-Democratic primary candidates Hillary Clinton and Bernie Sanders. He accused the former Secretary of State of colluding with the Democratic Party to prevent the Vermont congressman from becoming the party's presidential nominee. He resurrected that accusation when Sanders ran again in 2020.

Donald J. Trump ✔ @realDonaldTrump · Jun 25, 2017

Hillary Clinton colluded with the Democratic Party in order to beat Crazy Bernie Sanders. Is she allowed to so collude? Unfair to Bernie!

Donald J. Trump ✔ @realDonaldTrump · Apr 16, 2019

I believe it will be Crazy Bernie Sanders vs. Sleepy Joe Biden as the two finalists to run against maybe the best Economy in the history of our Country (and MANY other great things)! I look forward to facing whoever it may be. May God Rest Their Soul!

Donald J. Trump ✔ @realDonaldTrump · Jul 29, 2019

Crazy Bernie Sanders recently equated the City of Baltimore to a THIRD WORLD COUNTRY! Based on that statement, I assume that Bernie must now be labeled a Racist, just as a Republican would if he used that term and standard! The fact is, Baltimore can be brought back, maybe.

Donald J. Trump ✔ @realDonaldTrump · Jan 23, 2020

Crazy Bernie takes the lead in the Democrat Primaries, but it is looking more and more like the Dems will never allow him to win! Will Sleepy Joe be able to stumble across the finish line?

Donald J. Trump ✔ @realDonaldTrump · Feb 29, 2020

Democrats are working hard to destroy the name and reputation of Crazy Bernie Sanders, and take the nomination away from him!

SLEEPY JOE BIDEN

Pushing the narrative that former Vice President Joe Biden was suffering from cognitive decline during the 2020 election cycle, President Trump tweeted the nickname nearly 200 times to his 88.3 million Twitter followers. The president warned that if Biden was elected, Americans would suffer from massive tax hikes, a depression, and the loss of their Second Amendment rights.

Donald J. Trump ✔ @realDonaldTrump · Oct 12, 2020

The Economy is about ready to go through the roof. Stock Market ready to break ALL-TIME RECORD. 401k's incredible. New Jobs Record. Remember all of this when you VOTE. Sleepy Joe wants to quadruple your Taxes. Depression!!! Don't let it happen! #MAGA

Donald J. Trump ✔ @realDonaldTrump · Oct 17, 2020

SLEEPY JOE BIDEN IS PROPOSING THE BIGGEST TAX HIKE IN OUR COUNTRY'S HISTORY! CAN ANYBODY REALLY VOTE FOR THIS?

Donald J. Trump ✔ @realDonaldTrump · Oct 30, 2020

If Sleepy Joe Biden is actually elected President, the 4 Justices (plus1) that helped make such a ridiculous win possible would be relegated to sitting on not only a heavily PACKED COURT, but probably a REVOLVING COURT as well. At least the many new Justices will be Radical Left!

Donald J. Trump ✔ @realDonaldTrump · Nov 1, 2020

People are forgetting that if Sleepy Joe Biden and the Radical Left Dems win, you will vey quickly lose your Second Amendment!

Donald J. Trump ✔ @realDonaldTrump · Nov 2, 2020

Sleepy Joe Biden has vowed to ABOLISH the American oil and natural gas industries, and BAN fracking. Biden's energy ban will send every state into crushing poverty, from Michigan, to Wisconsin to Arizona to Pennsylvania.

A SOCIALIST NIGHTMARE

As the 2018 midterms approached, President Trump took to Twitter to warn his supporters that a vote for the Democratic Party was actually a vote for a variety of -isms: socialism, globalism, and communism, to name a few. He predicted via tweet that a Joe Biden presidency would lead to the dissolution of America's borders, the loss of gun rights, and the end of religious freedom.

Donald J. Trump ✔ @realDonaldTrump · Nov 5, 2018

Republicans have created the best economy in the HISTORY of our Country – and the hottest jobs market on planet earth. The Democrat Agenda is a Socialist Nightmare. The Republican Agenda is the AMERICAN DREAM!

Donald J. Trump ✔ @realDonaldTrump · Dec 20, 2019

I guess the magazine, "Christianity Today," is looking for Elizabeth Warren, Bernie Sanders, or those of the socialist/communist bent, to guard their religion. How about Sleepy Joe? The fact is, no President has ever done what I have done for Evangelicals, or religion itself!

Donald J. Trump ✔ @realDonaldTrump · Oct 15, 2020

Joe Biden and the Democrat Socialists will kill your jobs, dismantle your police departments, dissolve your borders, release criminal aliens, raise your taxes, confiscate your guns, end fracking, destroy your suburbs, and drive God from the public square.

Donald J. Trump ✔ @realDonaldTrump · Oct 29, 2020

This election is a choice between the AMERICAN DREAM and a SOCIALIST NIGHTMARE. Our opponents want to turn America into Communist Cuba or Socialist Venezuela. As long as I am President, America will NEVER be a socialist Country!

Donald J. Trump ✔ @realDonaldTrump · Nov 2, 2020

A vote for Sleepy Joe Biden is a vote to give control of government over to Globalists, Communists, Socialists, and Wealthy Liberal Hypocrites who want to silence, censor, cancel, and punish you. Get out and VOTE #MAGA tomorrow!

THE 2020 DEMOCRATIC PRIMARY

Like a sports commentator offering his opinion on a two-year-long boxing match, President Trump tweeted about the many candidates who fought to become the Democratic Party's 2020 nominee for president. From Beto and Bernie to Buttigieg and Bloomberg, the president proved he was prepared to insult whoever won what he referred to as the "Democrat Clown Show."

Donald J. Trump ✔ @realDonaldTrump · Jan 13, 2019

Best line in the Elizabeth Warren beer catastrophe is, to her husband, "Thank you for being here. I'm glad you're here" It's their house, he's supposed to be there!

Donald J. Trump ✔ @realDonaldTrump · Aug 6, 2019

Beto (phony name to indicate Hispanic heritage) O'Rourke, who is embarrassed by my last visit to the Great State of Texas, where I trounced him, and is now even more embarrassed by polling at 1% in the Democrat Primary, should respect the victims & law enforcement - & be quiet!

Donald J. Trump ✔ @realDonaldTrump · Oct 25, 2019

Another big dropout of the Presidential race was, along with 0% Tim Ryan, 0% @RepSwalwell. Such talk and bravado from both, and nothing to show. They stood for nothing, and the voters couldn't stand by them. Obnoxious and greedy politicians never make it in the end!

Donald J. Trump ✔ @realDonaldTrump · Feb 11, 2020

Bootedgeedge (Buttigieg) is doing pretty well tonight. Giving Crazy Bernie a run for his money. Very interesting!

Donald J. Trump ✔ @realDonaldTrump · Mar 1, 2020

Tom Steyer who, other than Mini Mike Bloomberg, spent more dollars for NOTHING than any candidate in history, quit the race today proclaiming how thrilled he was to be a part of the the Democrat Clown Show. Go away Tom and save whatever little money you have left!

JOE BIDEN'S BASEMENT

As COVID-19 shutdown the country and the 2020 election loomed ever nearer, President Trump blasted then-Democratic nominee Joe Biden for choosing to quarantine in his basement rather than campaign in person. While Biden interacted with voters and journalists online and on television, the president held large rallies everywhere from Minneapolis to Mosinee, Wisconsin.

 Donald J. Trump ✔ @realDonaldTrump · Jun 11, 2020

Sleepy Joe Biden refuses to leave his basement "sanctuary" and tell his Radical Left BOSSES that they are heading in the wrong direction. Tell them to get out of Seattle now. Liberal Governor @JayInslee is looking "the fool". LAW & ORDER!

 Donald J. Trump ✔ @realDonaldTrump · Aug 30, 2020

Joe Biden is coming out of the basement earlier than his hoped for ten days because his people told him he has no choice, his poll numbers are PLUNGING! Going to Pittsburgh, where I have helped industry to a record last year, & then back to his basement for an extended period.

 Donald J. Trump ✔ @realDonaldTrump · Sep 2, 2020

Joe Biden is a Low Energy Candidate the likes of which we have never seen before. The last thing our country needs is a Low Energy Individual, especially when surrounded by High Energy Chess Players scattered all over the world. He's back in his basement now - no schedule!

 Donald J. Trump ✔ @realDonaldTrump · Sep 3, 2020

Sleepy Joe Hiden' was acknowledged by his own people to have done a terrible job on a much easier situation, H1N1 Swine Flu. The OBiden Administration failed badly on this, & now he sits back in his basement and criticizes every move we make on the China Virus. DOING GREAT JOB!

 Donald J. Trump ✔ @realDonaldTrump · Sep 12, 2020

While I travel the Country, Joe sleeps in his basement, telling the Fake News Media to "get lost". If you're a reporter covering Sleepy Joe, you have basically gone into retirement!

OUR GREAT FIRST LADY

President Trump's wife Melania kept mostly out of the spotlight during his presidency but a handful of controversies arose anyway. The press alleged that Melania thought her husband would lose the 2016 election, criticized a jacket she wore, and speculated whether she was actually attending events with the president or if a doppelganger was being used in her place.

Donald J. Trump ✔ @realDonaldTrump · Nov 28, 2017

Melania, our great and very hard working First Lady, who truly loves what she is doing, always thought that "if you run, you will win." She would tell everyone that, "no doubt, he will win." I also felt I would win (or I would not have run) - and Country is doing great!

Donald J. Trump ✔ @realDonaldTrump · Jun 6, 2018

The Fake News Media has been so unfair, and vicious, to my wife and our great First Lady, Melania. During her recovery from surgery they reported everything from near death, to facelift, to left the W.H. (and me) for N.Y. or Virginia, to abuse. All Fake, she is doing really well!

Donald J. Trump ✔ @realDonaldTrump · Jun 21, 2018

"I REALLY DON'T CARE, DO U?" written on the back of Melania's jacket, refers to the Fake News Media. Melania has learned how dishonest they are, and she truly no longer cares!

Donald J. Trump ✔ @realDonaldTrump · Dec 4, 2018

Looking forward to being with the wonderful Bush family at Blair House today. The former First Lady will be coming over to the White House this morning to be given a tour of the Christmas decorations by Melania. The elegance & precision of the last two days have been remarkable!

Donald J. Trump ✔ @realDonaldTrump · Mar 13, 2019

The Fake News photoshopped pictures of Melania, then propelled conspiracy theories that it's actually not her by my side in Alabama and other places. They are only getting more deranged with time!

JARED & IVANKA

When President Trump appointed his daughter Ivanka and son-in-law Jared Kushner to positions in the executive branch, he became the first Commander in Chief to employ family members since President Kennedy appointed his brother to be attorney general in 1961. The president ignored the accusations of nepotism and happily welcomed his kids into the White House.

Donald J. Trump ✔ @realDonaldTrump · Jul 25, 2017

Jared Kushner did very well yesterday in proving he did not collude with the Russians. Witch Hunt. Next up, 11 year old Barron Trump!

Donald J. Trump ✔ @realDonaldTrump · Aug 2, 2018

They asked my daughter Ivanka whether or not the media is the enemy of the people. She correctly said no. It is the FAKE NEWS, which is a large percentage of the media, that is the enemy of the people!

Donald J. Trump ✔ @realDonaldTrump · Aug 30, 2018

Ivanka Trump & Jared Kushner had NOTHING to do with the so called "pushing out" of Don McGahn.The Fake News Media has it, purposely,so wrong! They love to portray chaos in the White House when they know that chaos doesn't exist-just a "smooth running machine" with changing parts!

Donald J. Trump ✔ @realDonaldTrump · Oct 12, 2018

So nice, everyone wants Ivanka Trump to be the new United Nations Ambassador. She would be incredible, but I can already hear the chants of Nepotism! We have great people that want the job.

Donald J. Trump ✔ @realDonaldTrump · Sep 28, 2020

Now Fake News @CNN is actually reporting that I wanted my daughter, Ivanka, to run with me as my Vice President in 2016 Election. Wrong and totally ridiculous. These people are sick!

PAUL RYAN

Wisconsin Republican Paul Ryan failed to escape the Twitter wrath of President Trump during his brief time as Speaker of the House. Ryan crossed the president in October 2018 when he publicly opposed the president's plan to end birthright citizenship with an executive order. President Trump slammed the congressman on Twitter and carried that grudge throughout his term.

Donald J. Trump ✔ @realDonaldTrump · Apr 11, 2018

Speaker Paul Ryan is a truly good man, and while he will not be seeking re-election, he will leave a legacy of achievement that nobody can question. We are with you Paul!

Donald J. Trump ✔ @realDonaldTrump · Oct 31, 2018

Paul Ryan should be focusing on holding the Majority rather than giving his opinions on Birthright Citizenship, something he knows nothing about! Our new Republican Majority will work on this, Closing the Immigration Loopholes and Securing our Border!

Donald J. Trump ✔ @realDonaldTrump · Jul 11, 2019

Paul Ryan, the failed V.P. candidate & former Speaker of the House, whose record of achievement was atrocious (except during my first two years as President), ultimately became a long running lame duck failure, leaving his Party in the lurch both as a fundraiser & leader.

Donald J. Trump ✔ @realDonaldTrump · Jul 13, 2019

Paul Ryan almost killed the Republican Party. Weak, ineffective & stupid are not exactly the qualities that Republicans, or the CITIZENS of our Country, were looking for. Right now our spirit is at an all time high, far better than the Radical Left Dems. You'll see next year!

Donald J. Trump ✔ @realDonaldTrump · Feb 20, 2020

Could somebody at @foxnews please explain to Trump hater A.B. Stoddard (zero talent!) and @TeamCavuto, that I won every one of my debates, from beginning to end. Check the polls taken immediately after the debates. The debates got me elected. Must be Fox Board Member Paul Ryan!

JEFF FLAKE & BOB CORKER

Few Republican senators spoke out against President Trump following his election in 2016, some because they respected and agreed with the president, others because they likely feared what tweets may await them if they did. Two senators, Jeff Flake and Bob Corker, found out early what would happen to Republicans who opposed the president. Both Congressmen retired soon after.

Donald J. Trump ✓ @realDonaldTrump · Oct 8, 2017

Senator Bob Corker "begged" me to endorse him for re-election in Tennessee. I said "NO" and he dropped out (said he could not win without my endorsement). He also wanted to be Secretary of State, I said "NO THANKS." He is also largely responsible for the horrendous Iran Deal!

Donald J. Trump ✓ @realDonaldTrump · Oct 25, 2017

The reason Flake and Corker dropped out of the Senate race is very simple, they had zero chance of being elected. Now act so hurt & wounded!

Donald J. Trump ✓ @realDonaldTrump · Oct 25, 2017

The meeting with Republican Senators yesterday, outside of Flake and Corker, was a love fest with standing ovations and great ideas for USA!

Donald J. Trump ✓ @realDonaldTrump · Jun 7, 2018

How could Jeff Flake, who is setting record low polling numbers in Arizona and was therefore humiliatingly forced out of his own Senate seat without even a fight (and who doesn't have a clue), think about running for office, even a lower one, again? Let's face it, he's a Flake!

Donald J. Trump ✓ @realDonaldTrump · Dec 23, 2018

Senator Bob Corker just stated that, "I'm so priveledged to serve in the Senate for twelve years, and that's what I told the people of our state that's what I'd do, serve for two terms." But that is Not True - wanted to run but poll numbers TANKED when I wouldn't endorse him.

MITT ROMNEY

President Trump endorsed former Republican presidential nominee Mitt Romney when he ran for one of Utah's senate seats in the 2018 midterms but soon found himself facing, as he tweeted, a RINO. After the senator publicly criticized the president's phone call with the Ukrainian president as "wrong and appalling," President Trump took to Twitter to call for Romney's impeachment.

 Donald J. Trump ✔ @realDonaldTrump · Feb 19, 2018

.@MittRomney has announced he is running for the Senate from the wonderful State of Utah. He will make a great Senator and worthy successor to @OrrinHatch, and has my full support and endorsement!

 Donald J. Trump ✔ @realDonaldTrump · Jan 2, 2019

Here we go with Mitt Romney, but so fast! Question will be, is he a Flake? I hope not. Would much prefer that Mitt focus on Border Security and so many other things where he can be helpful. I won big, and he didn't. He should be happy for all Republicans. Be a TEAM player & WIN!

 Donald J. Trump ✔ @realDonaldTrump · Oct 5, 2019

Mitt Romney never knew how to win. He is a pompous "ass" who has been fighting me from the beginning, except when he begged me for my endorsement for his Senate run (I gave it to him), and when he begged me to be Secretary of State (I didn't give it to him). He is so bad for R's!

 Donald J. Trump ✔ @realDonaldTrump · Oct 5, 2019

Somebody please wake up Mitt Romney and tell him that my conversation with the Ukrainian President was a congenial and very appropriate one, and my statement on China pertained to corruption, not politics. If Mitt worked this hard on Obama, he could have won. Sadly, he choked!

 Donald J. Trump ✔ @realDonaldTrump · Oct 5, 2019

I'm hearing that the Great People of Utah are considering their vote for their Pompous Senator, Mitt Romney, to be a big mistake. I agree! He is a fool who is playing right into the hands of the Do Nothing Democrats! #IMPEACHMITTROMNEY

MICHAEL COHEN

Following the release of secretly recorded conversations about hush money paid to a former Playboy model, a financial arrangement the president claimed to know nothing about, President Trump dismissed his former lawyer as a "rat." Cohen later pleaded guilty to lying to the FBI about the president's 2016 real estate dealings in Russia and served one year in federal prison.

Donald J. Trump ✔ @realDonaldTrump · Aug 22, 2018

If anyone is looking for a good lawyer, I would strongly suggest that you don't retain the services of Michael Cohen!

Donald J. Trump ✔ @realDonaldTrump · Dec 16, 2018

Remember, Michael Cohen only became a "Rat" after the FBI did something which was absolutely unthinkable & unheard of until the Witch Hunt was illegally started. They BROKE INTO AN ATTORNEY'S OFFICE! Why didn't they break into the DNC to get the Server, or Crooked's office?

Donald J. Trump ✔ @realDonaldTrump · Mar 1, 2019

Wow, just revealed that Michael Cohen wrote a "love letter to Trump" manuscript for a new book that he was pushing. Written and submitted long after Charlottesville and Helsinki, his phony reasons for going rogue. Book is exact opposite of his fake testimony, which now is a lie!

Donald J. Trump ✔ @realDonaldTrump · Mar 2, 2019

Virtually everything failed lawyer Michael Cohen said in his sworn testimony last week is totally contradicted in his just released manuscript for a book about me. It's a total new love letter to "Trump" and the pols must now use it rather than his lies for sentence reduction!

Donald J. Trump ✔ @realDonaldTrump · Mar 8, 2019

Bad lawyer and fraudster Michael Cohen said under sworn testimony that he never asked for a Pardon. His lawyers totally contradicted him. He lied! Additionally, he directly asked me for a pardon. I said NO. He lied again! He also badly wanted to work at the White House. He lied!

JEFF SESSIONS

Senator Jeff Sessions, an early supporter of President Trump's campaign, served as Attorney General for two years. During the Special Counsel investigation into Russia's attempts to influence the 2016 election, Sessions cited a conflict of interest and recused himself. The president tweeted his frustrations with that decision and eventually asked the AG to resign.

Donald J. Trump ✔ @realDonaldTrump · Mar 2, 2017

Jeff Sessions is an honest man. He did not say anything wrong. He could have stated his response more accurately, but it was clearly not intentional. This whole narrative is a way of saving face for Democrats losing an election that everyone thought they were supposed to win.

Donald J. Trump ✔ @realDonaldTrump · Feb 1, 2018

Question: If all of the Russian meddling took place during the Obama Administration, right up to January 20th, why aren't they the subject of the investigation? Why didn't Obama do something about the meddling? Why aren't Dem crimes under investigation? Ask Jeff Sessions!

Donald J. Trump ✔ @realDonaldTrump · Apr 21, 2018

The Washington Post said I refer to Jeff Sessions as "Mr. Magoo" and Rod Rosenstein as "Mr. Peepers." This is "according to people with whom the president has spoken." There are no such people and don't know these characters...just more Fake & Disgusting News to create ill will!

Donald J. Trump ✔ @realDonaldTrump · Jun 5, 2018

The Russian Witch Hunt Hoax continues, all because Jeff Sessions didn't tell me he was going to recuse himself...I would have quickly picked someone else. So much time and money wasted, so many lives ruined...and Sessions knew better than most that there was No Collusion!

Donald J. Trump ✔ @realDonaldTrump · Jun 3, 2020

Undercover Huber is a great spoof, funny, but at the same time sad, because the real @JohnWHuber did absolutely NOTHING. He was a garbage disposal unit for important documents & then, tap, tap, tap, just drag it along & run out of time. A.G. Jeff Sessions was played like a drum!

ROGER STONE

President Trump commuted the three-year federal prison sentence of former campaign advisor Roger Stone, who described the president's election win as a "manifestation of a dream I've had since 1988" in the documentary "Get Me Roger Stone," after Stone was convicted of lying to Congress during the investigation into Russia's attempts to influence the 2016 election.

Donald J. Trump ✔ @realDonaldTrump · Dec 3, 2018

"I will never testify against Trump." This statement was recently made by Roger Stone, essentially stating that he will not be forced by a rogue and out of control prosecutor to make up lies and stories about "President Trump." Nice to know that some people still have "guts!"

Donald J. Trump ✔ @realDonaldTrump · Jan 26, 2019

If Roger Stone was indicted for lying to Congress, what about the lying done by Comey, Brennan, Clapper, Lisa Page & lover, Baker and soooo many others? What about Hillary to FBI and her 33,000 deleted Emails? What about Lisa & Peter's deleted texts & Wiener's laptop? Much more!

Donald J. Trump ✔ @realDonaldTrump · Feb 12, 2020

Two months in jail for a Swamp Creature, yet 9 years recommended for Roger Stone (who was not even working for the Trump Campaign). Gee, that sounds very fair! Rogue prosecutors maybe? The Swamp! @foxandfriends @TuckerCarlson

Donald J. Trump ✔ @realDonaldTrump · Feb 25, 2020

There has rarely been a juror so tainted as the forewoman in the Roger Stone case. Look at her background. She never revealed her hatred of "Trump" and Stone. She was totally biased, as is the judge. Roger wasn't even working on my campaign. Miscarriage of justice. Sad to watch!

Donald J. Trump ✔ @realDonaldTrump · Jun 4, 2020

No. Roger was a victim of a corrupt and illegal Witch Hunt, one which will go down as the greatest political crime in history. He can sleep well at night!

RUDY GIULIANI

Former New York City mayor and lawyer Rudy Giuliani began representing President Trump in court in 2018. He led the legal charge to overturn the results of the 2020 election and, as a result, had his license to practice law revoked by a panel of justices who determined that Giuliani had made "demonstrably false and misleading statements to courts, lawmakers, and the public."

Donald J. Trump ✓ @realDonaldTrump · Sep 11, 2018

Rudy Giuliani did a GREAT job as Mayor of NYC during the period of September 11th. His leadership, bravery and skill must never be forgotten. Rudy is a TRUE WARRIOR!

Donald J. Trump ✓ @realDonaldTrump · Oct 12, 2019

So now they are after the legendary "crime buster" and greatest Mayor in the history of NYC, Rudy Giuliani. He may seem a little rough around the edges sometimes, but he is also a great guy and wonderful lawyer. Such a one sided Witch Hunt going on in USA. Deep State. Shameful!

Donald J. Trump ✓ @realDonaldTrump · Mar 1, 2020

Mini Mike Bloomberg didn't bring NYC back, as he said in his fake ad. It was @RudyGiuliani who brought NYC back and who also, with his endorsement, got Mini Mike elected (with barely a thank you). A boring mayor who the people couldn't stand!

Donald J. Trump ✓ @realDonaldTrump · Nov 14, 2020

I look forward to Mayor Giuliani spearheading the legal effort to defend OUR RIGHT to FREE and FAIR ELECTIONS! Rudy Giuliani, Joseph diGenova, Victoria Toensing, Sidney Powell, and Jenna Ellis, a truly great team, added to our other wonderful lawyers and representatives!

Donald J. Trump ✓ @realDonaldTrump · Dec 6, 2020

.@RudyGiuliani, by far the greatest mayor in the history of NYC, and who has been working tirelessly exposing the most corrupt election (by far!) in the history of the USA, has tested positive for the China Virus. Get better soon Rudy, we will carry on!!!

PAUL MANAFORT

Paul Manafort, who chaired the president's campaign in the summer of 2016, pleaded guilty to charges of conspiracy to defraud the United States and witness tampering and was sentenced to 47 months in federal prison. Manafort spent two years behind bars before President Trump, who championed Manafort on Twitter, issued him a full pardon in the final month of his presidency.

Donald J. Trump ✔ @realDonaldTrump · Jun 3, 2018

As only one of two people left who could become President, why wouldn't the FBI or Department of "Justice" have told me that they were secretly investigating Paul Manafort (on charges that were 10 years old and had been previously dropped) during my campaign? Should have told me!

Donald J. Trump ✔ @realDonaldTrump · Jun 3, 2018

Paul Manafort came into the campaign very late and was with us for a short period of time (he represented Ronald Reagan, Bob Dole & many others over the years), but we should have been told that Comey and the boys were doing a number on him, and he wouldn't have been hired!

Donald J. Trump ✔ @realDonaldTrump · Aug 1, 2018

Looking back on history, who was treated worse, Alfonse Capone, legendary mob boss, killer and "Public Enemy Number One," or Paul Manafort, political operative & Reagan/Dole darling, now serving solitary confinement - although convicted of nothing? Where is the Russian Collusion?

Donald J. Trump ✔ @realDonaldTrump · Aug 22, 2018

I feel very badly for Paul Manafort and his wonderful family. "Justice" took a 12 year old tax case, among other things, applied tremendous pressure on him and, unlike Michael Cohen, he refused to "break" - make up stories in order to get a "deal." Such respect for a brave man!

Donald J. Trump ✔ @realDonaldTrump · Feb 11, 2018

Is this the Judge that put Paul Manafort in SOLITARY CONFINEMENT, something that not even mobster Al Capone had to endure? How did she treat Crooked Hillary Clinton? Just asking!

BRETT KAVANAUGH

Justice Brett Kavanaugh, President Trump's second successful nomination to the Supreme Court, faced accusations of sexual assault, which he adamantly denied, during his confirmation process. The president stood by his nominee and lashed out at the haters on Twitter until Kavanaugh was confirmed by the Republican-controlled Senate with a 50-48 vote along (mostly) party lines.

Donald J. Trump @realDonaldTrump · Sep 4, 2018

The Brett Kavanaugh hearings for the future Justice of the Supreme Court are truly a display of how mean, angry, and despicable the other side is. They will say anything, and are only looking to inflict pain and embarrassment to one of the most highly renowned jurists to ever appear before Congress. So sad to see!

Donald J. Trump @realDonaldTrump · Sep 21, 2018

Judge Brett Kavanaugh is a fine man, with an impeccable reputation, who is under assault by radical left wing politicians who don't want to know the answers, they just want to destroy and delay. Facts don't matter. I go through this with them every single day in D.C.

Donald J. Trump @realDonaldTrump · Oct 3, 2018

I see it each time I go out to Rallies in order to help some of our great Republican candidates. VOTERS ARE REALLY ANGRY AT THE VICIOUS AND DESPICABLE WAY DEMOCRATS ARE TREATING BRETT KAVANAUGH! He and his wonderful family deserve much better.

Donald J. Trump @realDonaldTrump · Sep 15, 2019

Now the Radical Left Democrats and their Partner, the LameStream Media, are after Brett Kavanaugh again, talking loudly of their favorite word, impeachment. He is an innocent man who has been treated HORRIBLY. Such lies about him. They want to scare him into turning Liberal!

Donald J. Trump @realDonaldTrump · Sep 15, 2019

Brett Kavanaugh should start suing people for libel, or the Justice Department should come to his rescue. The lies being told about him are unbelievable. False Accusations without recrimination. When does it stop? They are trying to influence his opinions. Can't let that happen!

THE MOOCH

Anthony Scaramucci, a former Wall Street financier and early backer of President Trump during the 2016 election, served as White House Communications Director for precisely 10 days. The Mooch was the third of five people to hold the position during the president's term. After his dismissal, he became a vocal critic of the president and endorsed Joe Biden in the 2020 election.

Donald J. Trump ✔ @realDonaldTrump · Aug 10, 2019

Anthony Scaramucci, who was quickly terminated (11 days) from a position that he was totally incapable of handling, now seems to do nothing but television as the all time expert on "President Trump." Like many other so-called television experts, he knows very little about me.

Donald J. Trump ✔ @realDonaldTrump · Aug 12, 2019

Scaramucci, who like so many others had nothing to do with my Election victory, is only upset that I didn't want him back in the Administration (where he desperately wanted to be). Also, I seldom had time to return his many calls to me. He just wanted to be on TV!

Donald J. Trump ✔ @realDonaldTrump · Aug 19, 2019

Anthony Scaramucci is a highly unstable "nut job" who was with other candidates in the primary who got shellacked, & then unfortunately wheedled his way into my campaign. I barely knew him until his 11 days of gross incompetence-made a fool of himself, bad on TV. Abused staff, got fired.

Donald J. Trump ✔ @realDonaldTrump · Aug 9, 2020

.@Scaramucci, who just made a fool of himself as he got taken apart by @SteveHiltonx, only lasted 11 days in his favorite of all time Administration, before being fired for, again, making a fool of himself. Anthony is a loser who begged to come back. I said "No Thanks".

Donald J. Trump ✔ @realDonaldTrump · Oct 16, 2020

Steve Scully of @cspan had a very bad week. When his name was announced, I said he would not be appropriate because of conflicts. I was right! Then he said he was hacked, he wasn't. I was right again! But his biggest mistake was "confiding" in a lowlife loser like the Mooch. Sad!

BEN SASSE

Nebraska's Ben Sasse found himself in President Trump's Twitter crosshairs following critical comments he made about the president's leadership, handling of the COVID-19 pandemic, and much more during a public town hall with constituents. The president suggested that, perhaps like Senators Jeff Flake and Bob Corker, Sasse would soon be forced to retire from politics.

Donald J. Trump ✔ @realDonaldTrump · Aug 10, 2020

RINO Ben Sasse, who needed my support and endorsement in order to get the Republican nomination for Senate from the GREAT State of Nebraska, has, now that he's got it (Thank you President T), gone rogue, again. This foolishness plays right into the hands of the Radical Left Dems!

Donald J. Trump ✔ @realDonaldTrump · Oct 17, 2020

The least effective of our 53 Republican Senators, and a person who truly doesn't have what it takes to be great, is Little Ben Sasse of Nebraska, a State which I have gladly done so much to help. @SenSasse was as nice as a RINO can be until he recently won the Republican....

Donald J. Trump ✔ @realDonaldTrump · Oct 17, 2020

...Nomination to run for a second term. Then he went back to his rather stupid and obnoxious ways. Must feel he can't lose to a Dem. Little Ben is a liability to the Republican Party, and an embarrassment to the Great State of Nebraska. Other than that, he's just a wonderful guy!

Donald J. Trump ✔ @realDonaldTrump · Oct 17, 2020

Senator Little Ben Sasse of the Great State of Nebraska seems to be heading down the same inglorious path as former Senators Liddle' Bob Corker, whose approval rating in Tennessee went from 55% to 4%, & Jeff "the Flake" Flake, whose approval rating in Arizona went from 56% to....

Donald J. Trump ✔ @realDonaldTrump · Oct 17, 2020

....practically nothing. Both Senators became totally unelectable, couldn't come even close to winning their primaries, and decided to drop out of politics and gracefully "RETIRE". @SenSasse could be next, or perhaps the Republicans should find a new and more viable candidate?

JOHN BOLTON

After Generals Michael Flynn and H.R. McMaster both resigned from the role of National Security Advisor, longtime Republican John Bolton became the third person to take on the position. A year later, Bolton either resigned (if you believe his telling of events) or was fired (if you believe the tweet) following an increasingly strained relationship with the president over foreign policy.

Donald J. Trump ✓ @realDonaldTrump · Jun 22, 2020

I gave John Bolton, who was incapable of being Senate confirmed because he was considered a wacko, and was not liked, a chance. I always like hearing differing points of view. He turned out to be grossly incompetent, and a liar. See judge's opinion. CLASSIFIED INFORMATION!!!

Donald J. Trump ✓ @realDonaldTrump · Jun 23, 2020

Washed up Creepster John Bolton is a lowlife who should be in jail, money seized, for disseminating, for profit, highly Classified information. Remember what they did to the young submarine sailor, but did nothing to Crooked Hillary. I ended up pardoning him - It wasn't fair!

Donald J. Trump ✓ @realDonaldTrump · Sep 7, 2020

Just heard that Wacko John Bolton was talking of the fact that I discussed "love letters from Kim Jong Un" as though I viewed them as just that. Obviously, was just being sarcastic. Bolton was such a jerk!

Donald J. Trump ✓ @realDonaldTrump · Nov 15, 2020

John Bolton was one of the dumbest people in government that I've had the "pleasure" to work with. A sullen, dull and quiet guy, he added nothing to National Security except, "Gee, let's go to war." Also, illegally released much Classified Information. A real dope!

Donald J. Trump ✓ @realDonaldTrump · Dec 20, 2020

What would Bolton, one of the dumbest people in Washington, know? Wasn't he the person who so stupidly said, on television, "Libyan solution", when describing what the U.S. was going to do for North Korea? I've got plenty of other Bolton "stupid stories".

TRUMP HATERS

President Trump often dismissed people who were critical of his actions, words, and policy decisions as "Trump haters," suggesting that their opposition to his agenda was more of a political grudge than a genuine disagreement over the issues. Unless explicitly supportive of the president at every turn, politicians and journalists ran the risk of being labeled a hater on Twitter.

Donald J. Trump ✓ @realDonaldTrump · Jun 26, 2018

Wow! Big Trump Hater Congressman Joe Crowley, who many expected was going to take Nancy Pelosi's place, just LOST his primary election. In other words, he's out! That is a big one that nobody saw happening. Perhaps he should have been nicer, and more respectful, to his President!

Donald J. Trump ✓ @realDonaldTrump · Dec 16, 2019

The problem is that the so-called Commission on Presidential Debates is stacked with Trump Haters & Never Trumpers. 3 years ago they were forced to publicly apologize for modulating my microphone in the first debate against Crooked Hillary. As President, the debates are up to me, and there are many options.

Donald J. Trump ✓ @realDonaldTrump · May 5, 2020

Wow! Congratulations to Greg Gutfeld, a one time Trump Hater who has come all the way home. His Ratings easily beat no talent Stephen Colbert, nice guy Jimmy Fallon, and wacko "last placer" Jimmy Kimmel. Greg built his show from scratch, and did a great job in doing so. @FoxNews

Donald J. Trump ✓ @realDonaldTrump · Sept 10, 2020

Now @FoxNews is putting on yet another loser, Jamie Weinstein, into their stable of Trump haters. People who failed for many years are now going on Fox to explain "Trump". Schumer puppet Chris Hahn and his twin brother, Richard Goodstein, together with cheater Donna Brazil. Bad!

Donald J. Trump ✓ @realDonaldTrump · Sep 17, 2020

Bob Woodward's badly written book is very boring & totally "obsolete". Didn't even talk about the recent Middle East deal. Just another tired, washed up Trump Hater, who can't stand that I have done so much, so quickly! #MAGA

LOSERS

Given his history of calling people "losers," including former Republican senator and Vietnam War veteran John McCain, it was difficult for President Trump to deny accusations that he'd used the same insult to refer to Marines buried in a World War II cemetery in France in 2020. On Twitter, the president categorized Hillary Clinton, terrorists, the mainstream media, and more as losers.

Donald J. Trump @realDonaldTrump · Mar 20, 2019

George Conway, often referred to as Mr. Kellyanne Conway by those who know him, is VERY jealous of his wife's success & angry that I, with her help, didn't give him the job he so desperately wanted. I barely know him but just take a look, a stone cold LOSER & husband from hell!

Donald J. Trump @realDonaldTrump · Jun 3, 2019

.@SadiqKhan, who by all accounts has done a terrible job as Mayor of London, has been foolishly "nasty" to the visiting President of the United States, by far the most important ally of the United Kingdom. He is a stone cold loser who should focus on crime in London, not me

Donald J. Trump @realDonaldTrump · May 5, 2020

Crazed Rick Wilson lost for Evan "McMuffin" McMullin (to me). Steve Schmidt & Reed Galvin lost for John McCain, Romney's campaign manager (?) lost big to "O", & Jennifer Horn got thrown out of the New Hampshire Republican Party. They're all LOSERS, but Abe Lincoln, Republican, is all smiles!

Donald J. Trump @realDonaldTrump · Oct 13, 2020

How dare failed Presidential Candidate (1% and falling!) @CoryBooker make false charges and statements about me in addressing Judge Barrett. Illegally, never even lived in Newark when he was Mayor. Guy is a total loser! I want better Healthcare for far less money, always.

Donald J. Trump @realDonaldTrump · Nov 25, 2020

The "losers & suckers" statement on dead military heroes has been proven to be a total fabrication and lie. IT WAS NEVER MADE! The "anonymous" fabricator, who is a major sleaze, went forward with the lie despite 25 strong witnesses to the contrary. Welcome to the roaring 20's!

LIGHTWEIGHTS

"Lightweight," defined as being of little to no consequence or ability, was the 45th president's chosen insult for a select few senators and journalists and one lucky mayor. Unlike the agreeable Republicans President Trump lauded as "strong" and "tough," lightweights were described as begging for campaign contributions and quitting social media after being called mean names.

Donald J. Trump ✓ @realDonaldTrump · Dec 12, 2017

Lightweight Senator Kirsten Gillibrand, a total flunky for Chuck Schumer and someone who would come to my office "begging" for campaign contributions not so long ago (and would do anything for them), is now in the ring fighting against Trump. Very disloyal to Bill & Crooked-USED!

Donald J. Trump ✓ @realDonaldTrump · Aug 28, 2019

"The infestation of bedbugs at The New York Times office" @OANN was perhaps brought in by lightweight journalist Bret Stephens, a Conservative who does anything that his bosses at the paper tell him to do! He is now quitting Twitter after being called a "bedbug." Tough guy!

Donald J. Trump ✓ @realDonaldTrump · Sep 7, 2019

The Washington Post's @PhilipRucker (Mr. Off the Record) & @AshleyRParker, two nasty lightweight reporters, shouldn't even be allowed on the grounds of the White House because their reporting is so DISGUSTING & FAKE. Also, add the appointment of MANY Federal Judges this Summer!

Donald J. Trump ✓ @realDonaldTrump · Jan 26, 2020

Paul Krugman is a lightweight thinker who doesn't have a clue. Caused huge economic damage to his follower's pocketbooks. He, and others, should be fired by @nytimes!

Donald J. Trump ✓ @realDonaldTrump · Feb 9, 2020

So good to see that Republicans will be winning the Great State of Alabama Senate Seat back, now that lightweight Senator @DougJones cast a partisan vote for the Impeachment Hoax. Thought his boss, Cryin' Chuck, would have forced him to vote against the Hoax. A Do Nothing Stiff!

CLOWNS

Though not as prevalent as haters, losers, and fools, "clowns" made an occasional appearance on the president's Twitter account. President Trump used this particular insult to refer to certain members of the FBI, Special Counsel Robert Mueller and his investigative team, the numerous 2020 Democratic primary candidates, and the governor of Georgia following the 2020 election.

Donald J. Trump ✔ @realDonaldTrump · Aug 11, 2018

Will the FBI ever recover it's once stellar reputation, so badly damaged by Comey, McCabe, Peter S and his lover, the lovely Lisa Page, and other top officials now dismissed or fired? So many of the great men and women of the FBI have been hurt by these clowns and losers!

Donald J. Trump ✔ @realDonaldTrump · Jul 27, 2019

Robert Mueller's testimony, and the Mueller Report itself, was a disaster for this illegal Democrat inspired Witch Hunt. It is an embarrassment to the USA that they don't know how to stop. They can't help themselves, they are totally lost, they are Clowns!

Donald J. Trump ✔ @realDonaldTrump · Oct 16, 2019

Our record Economy would CRASH, just like in 1929, if any of those clowns became President!

Donald J. Trump ✔ @realDonaldTrump · Jan 23, 2020

By doing this, he figures, they won't hit him as hard during his hopeless "presidential" campaign. They will remain silent! The fact is, when Mini losses, he will be spending very little of his money on these "clowns" because he will consider himself to be the biggest clown of them all - and he will be right!

Donald J. Trump ✔ @realDonaldTrump · Dec 14, 2020

What a fool Governor @BrianKempGA of Georgia is. Could have been so easy, but now we have to do it the hard way. Demand this clown call a Special Session and open up signature verification, NOW. Otherwise, could be a bad day for two GREAT Senators on January 5th.

NEVER TRUMPERS

Republicans who spoke out against the president were sometimes dubbed "Never Trumpers," regardless of whether they had participated in the actual Never Trump movement during the 2016 election or not. These Republicans, President Trump tweeted in warning, were "worse and more dangerous" than the Democrats. He even went so far as to refer to them as "human scum."

Donald J. Trump ✔ @realDonaldTrump · Oct 23, 2019

The Never Trumper Republicans, though on respirators with not many left, are in certain ways worse and more dangerous for our Country than the Do Nothing Democrats. Watch out for them, they are human scum!

Donald J. Trump ✔ @realDonaldTrump · Oct 23, 2019

It would be really great if the people within the Trump Administration, all well-meaning and good (I hope!), could stop hiring Never Trumpers, who are worse than the Do Nothing Democrats. Nothing good will ever come from them!

Donald J. Trump ✔ @realDonaldTrump · Nov 17, 2019

Tell Jennifer Williams, whoever that is, to read BOTH transcripts of the presidential calls, & see the just released ststement from Ukraine. Then she should meet with the other Never Trumpers, who I don't know & mostly never even heard of, & work out a better presidential attack!

Donald J. Trump ✔ @realDonaldTrump · Oct 9, 2020

.@SteveScully, the Never Trumper next debate moderator, got caught cold. Pulled out the old, "I've been hacked", line. That never works. His bosses are furious at him as he's lost all credibility!

Donald J. Trump ✔ @realDonaldTrump · Dec 7, 2020

Georgia Lt. Governor @GeoffDuncanGA is a RINO Never Trumper who got himself elected as LG by falsely claiming to be "pro-Trump". Too dumb or corrupt to recognize massive evidence of fraud in GA & should be replaced! We need every great Georgian to call him out! #SpecialSession!

LOW IQ INDIVIDUALS

A longtime fan of insulting other people's intelligence, President Trump continued that tradition during his presidency, accusing Fox News anchors, Robert De Niro, and, of course, Democratic candidate Joe Biden of having a low IQ. Sometimes he dumbed down the insult, tweeting that certain people, like billionaire Mark Cuban and Slippery James Comey, were just "not smart."

Donald J. Trump ✓ @realDonaldTrump · Jun 25, 2018

Congresswoman Maxine Waters, an extraordinarily low IQ person, has become, together with Nancy Pelosi, the Face of the Democrat Party. She has just called for harm to supporters, of which there are many, of the Make America Great Again movement. Be careful what you wish for Max!

Donald J. Trump ✓ @realDonaldTrump · Aug 30, 2018

North Korea fired off some small weapons, which disturbed some of my people, and others, but not me. I have confidence that Chairman Kim will keep his promise to me, & also smiled when he called Swampman Joe Biden a low IQ individual, & worse. Perhaps that's sending me a signal?

Donald J. Trump ✓ @realDonaldTrump · Oct 16, 2018

Elizabeth Warren is being hammered, even by the Left. Her false claim of Indian heritage is only selling to VERY LOW I.Q. individuals!

Donald J. Trump ✓ @realDonaldTrump · Jun 28, 2020

THE VAST SILENT MAJORITY IS ALIVE AND WELL!!! We will win this Election big. Nobody wants a Low IQ person in charge of our Country, and Sleepy Joe is definitely a Low IQ person!

Donald J. Trump ✓ @realDonaldTrump · Oct 7, 2020

He's been a wacko for years, and everyone knows it. The Lamestream Media is stuck with him and they are just now trying to clean up his act. Notice how all of the bad things, like his very low IQ, are no longer reported? Fake News! #MAGA

FOOLS & FOOLISHNESS

The president condemned those who criticized his Make America Great Again agenda as "fools," suggesting they were simply not intelligent enough to understand the brilliance of his plans. Other foolish things, according to President Trump's tweets, included not abolishing the senate filibuster, past trade deals with China, and not capturing 9/11 terrorist Osama Bin Laden sooner.

Donald J. Trump ✔ @realDonaldTrump · Jul 29, 2017

Republicans in the Senate will NEVER win if they don't go to a 51 vote majority NOW. They look like fools and are just wasting time.

Donald J. Trump ✔ @realDonaldTrump · Aug 17, 2017

Sad to see the history and culture of our great country being ripped apart with the removal of our beautiful statues and monuments. You can't change history, but you can learn from it. Robert E Lee, Stonewall Jackson - who's next, Washington, Jefferson? So foolish!

Donald J. Trump ✔ @realDonaldTrump · Nov 19, 2018

Of course we should have captured Osama Bin Laden long before we did. I pointed him out in my book just BEFORE the attack on the World Trade Center. President Clinton famously missed his shot. We paid Pakistan Billions of Dollars & they never told us he was living there. Fools!

Donald J. Trump ✔ @realDonaldTrump · Jul 26, 2019

France just put a digital tax on our great American technology companies. If anybody taxes them, it should be their home Country, the USA. We will announce a substantial reciprocal action on Macron's foolishness shortly. I've always said American wine is better than French wine!

Donald J. Trump ✔ @realDonaldTrump · Jan 18, 2020

A massive 200 Billion Dollar Sea Wall, built around New York to protect it from rare storms, is a costly, foolish & environmentally unfriendly idea that, when needed, probably won't work anyway. It will also look terrible. Sorry, you'll just have to get your mops & buckets ready!

TRUMP TWEETS ABOUT... THE HATERS
PSYCHOS

President Trump's favorite "psycho," for whom he almost exclusively reserved the insult, was MSNBC anchor Joe Scarborough. The president lost interest in the host following his 2016 election win and eventually used his large Twitter platform to suggest Scarborough had been personally involved in the accidental death of a young staffer in his political office 20 years earlier.

Donald J. Trump ✔ @realDonaldTrump · Apr 21, 2020

Watched the first 5 minutes of poorly rated Morning Psycho on MSDNC just to see if he is as "nuts" as people are saying. He's worse. Such hatred and contempt! I used to do his show all the time before the 2016 election, then cut him off. Wasn't worth the effort, his mind is shot!

Donald J. Trump ✔ @realDonaldTrump · May 4, 2020

"Concast" should open up a long overdue Florida Cold Case against Psycho Joe Scarborough. I know him and Crazy Mika well, used them beautifully in the last Election, dumped them nicely, and will state on the record that he is "nuts". Besides, bad ratings! #OPENJOECOLDCASE

Donald J. Trump ✔ @realDonaldTrump · May 12, 2020

When will they open a Cold Case on the Psycho Joe Scarborough matter in Florida. Did he get away with murder? Some people think so. Why did he leave Congress so quietly and quickly? Isn't it obvious? What's happening now? A total nut job!

Donald J. Trump ✔ @realDonaldTrump · May 24, 2020

A lot of interest in this story about Psycho Joe Scarborough. So a young marathon runner just happened to faint in his office, hit her head on his desk, & die? I would think there is a lot more to this story than that? An affair? What about the so-called investigator?

Donald J. Trump ✔ @realDonaldTrump · May 27, 2020

Psycho Joe Scarborough is rattled, not only by his bad ratings but all of the things and facts that are coming out on the internet about opening a Cold Case. He knows what is happening!

LOWLIFES

In general, "lowlifes" were people the president had, at one point in time or another, suggested were worthy of investigation, resignation or firing, and/or treason or jailtime. It wasn't a common insult – President Trump tweeted it just 17 times during his presidency — but he appeared to find it useful when describing former White House officials, reporters, FBI members, and protesters.

Donald J. Trump ✔ @realDonaldTrump · Apr 13, 2018

While I know it's "not presidential" to take on a lowlife like Omarosa, and while I would rather not be doing so, this is a modern day form of communication and I know the Fake News Media will be working overtime to make even Wacky Omarosa look legitimate as possible. Sorry!

Donald J. Trump ✔ @realDonaldTrump · Aug 14, 2018

When you give a crazed, crying lowlife a break, and give her a job at the White House, I guess it just didn't work out. Good work by General Kelly for quickly firing that dog!

Donald J. Trump ✔ @realDonaldTrump · Oct 2, 2019

Adam Schiff should only be so lucky to have the brains, honor and strength of Secretary of State Mike Pompeo. For a lowlife like Schiff, who completely fabricated my words and read them to Congress as though they were said by me, to demean a First in Class at West Point, is SAD!

Donald J. Trump ✔ @realDonaldTrump · Jun 23, 2020

It is ashame that Congress doesn't do something about the lowlifes that burn the American Flag. It should be stopped, and now!

Donald J. Trump ✔ @realDonaldTrump · Jul 24, 2020

So Obama and his team of lowlifes spied on my campaign, and got caught - Open and shut case! More papers released today which are devastating to them. Will they ever pay the price? The political Crime of the Century!

DISASTERS

President Trump occasionally labeled Democratic politicians "disasters," especially while they were campaigning for office. Non-human disasters, according to the president's tweets, included the Affordable Care Act, U.S. immigration and trade policies, and what he predicted would have happened to the economy, taxes, and more had Democrats won the 2016 presidential election.

Donald J. Trump ✔ @realDonaldTrump · Oct 22, 2017

Wacky Congresswoman Wilson is the gift that keeps on giving for the Republican Party, a disaster for Dems. You watch her in action & vote R!

Donald J. Trump ✔ @realDonaldTrump · Apr 14, 2019

Such a "puff piece" on Nancy Pelosi by @60minutes, yet her leadership has passed no meaningful Legislation. All they do is Investigate, as it turns out, crimes that they instigated & committed. The Mueller No Collusion decision wasn't even discussed- and she was a disaster at W.H.

Donald J. Trump ✔ @realDonaldTrump · Oct 18, 2019

Susan Rice, who was a disaster to President Obama as National Security Advisor, is now telling us her opinion on what to do in Syria. Remember RED LINE IN THE SAND? That was Obama. Millions killed! No thanks Susan, you were a disaster.

Donald J. Trump ✔ @realDonaldTrump · Apr 17, 2020

Biden/Obama were a disaster in handling the H1N1 Swine Flu. Polling at the time showed disastrous approval numbers. 17,000 people died unnecessarily and through incompetence! Also, don't forget their 5 Billion Dollar Obamacare website that should have cost close to nothing!

Donald J. Trump ✔ @realDonaldTrump · Oct 27, 2020

They (his handlers) ripped Sleepy Joe off the stage yesterday when he got lost in a "mental fog". A disaster. Very little reporting on this!

RINOS

RINO, short for "Republican in name only," is an acronym that gained popularity in the mid-1990s, and President Trump made quite a few RINO sightings during his term in the Oval Office. The president fired off disapproving tweets whenever Republicans spoke out against him, often denouncing them as "weak" and questioning why they were working to undermine his agenda.

Donald J. Trump ✓ @realDonaldTrump · May 5, 2020

Most of the money raised by the RINO losers of the so-called "Lincoln Project", goes into their own pockets. With what I've done on Judges, Taxes, Regulations, Healthcare, the Military, Vets (Choice!) & protecting our great 2A, they should love Trump. Problem is, I BEAT THEM ALL!

Donald J. Trump ✓ @realDonaldTrump · Jun 29, 2020

95% Approval Rating of President Trump in the Republican Party. I would imagine the 5% are the RINOS' and stupid people who don't want to see great Judges & Supreme Court Justice's, a new & powerful Military, Choice for Vets, 2A Protection, big RegulationCuts, Life, & much more!

Donald J. Trump ✓ @realDonaldTrump · Jul 11, 2020

Do RINO'S Pat Toomey & Mitt Romney have any problem with the fact that we caught Obama, Biden, & Company illegally spying on my campaign? Do they care if Comey, McCabe, Page & her lover, Peter S, the whole group, ran rampant, wild & unchecked - lying & leaking all the way? NO!

Donald J. Trump ✓ @realDonaldTrump · Jul 23, 2020

Recently watched failed RINO Tom Ridge, former head of Homeland Security, trying to justify his sudden love of the Radical Left Mayor of Portland, who last night was booed & shouted out of existence by the agitators & anarchists. Love watching pathetic Never Trumpers squirm!

Donald J. Trump ✓ @realDonaldTrump · Jan 5, 2021

I hope the Democrats, and even more importantly, the weak and ineffective RINO section of the Republican Party, are looking at the thousands of people pouring into D.C. They won't stand for a landslide election victory to be stolen. @senatemajldr @JohnCornyn @SenJohnThune

THE DUMBEST

Occasionally, President Trump took his "low IQ individual" insult to the next level, describing some people not just as dumb but as "the dumbest." He also tossed the insult "dumb as a rock" at former Secretary of State Rex Tillerson, who was fired via tweet, and Congresswoman Alexandria Ocasio-Cortez, a vocal leader of the Democratic Party's most liberal faction.

Donald J. Trump ✔ @realDonaldTrump · Dec 11, 2017

Another false story, this time in the Failing @nytimes, that I watch 4-8 hours of television a day - Wrong! Also, I seldom, if ever, watch CNN or MSNBC, both of which I consider Fake News. I never watch Don Lemon, who I once called the "dumbest man on television!" Bad Reporting.

Donald J. Trump ✔ @realDonaldTrump · May 23, 2019

Rex Tillerson, a man who is "dumb as a rock" and totally ill prepared and ill equipped to be Secretary of State, made up a story (he got fired) that I was out-prepared by Vladimir Putin at a meeting in Hamburg, Germany. I don't think Putin would agree. Look how the U.S. is doing!

Donald J. Trump ✔ @realDonaldTrump · Apr 30, 2020

I must admit that Lyin' Brian Williams is, while dumber than hell, quite a bit smarter than Fake News @CNN "anchorman" Don Lemon, the "dumbest man on television". Then you have Psycho Joe "What Ever Happened To Your Girlfriend?" Scarborough, another of the low I.Q. individuals!

Donald J. Trump ✔ @realDonaldTrump · May 22, 2020

.@deanbaquet is to be seriously respected. He has long been considered one of the dumbest men in the world of journalism, and he became Executive Editor of the Failing New York Times. Not easy to do. He has given up on "figuring Trump out". Called it all wrong from the beginning, was forced to apologize (Fake News!).

Donald J. Trump ✔ @realDonaldTrump · Dec 20, 2020

What would Bolton, one of the dumbest people in Washington, know? Wasn't he the person who so stupidly said, on television, "Libyan solution", when describing what the U.S. was going to do for North Korea? I've got plenty of other Bolton "stupid stories".

THE WORST

The 45th president, highly skilled in hyperbole, referred to someone or something as "the worst" in 76 different tweets during his term in the Oval Office. Sometimes he referred to trade deals and economic policies, other times the Emmys and Democratic mayors. Each time, President Trump stressed to his Twitter followers how terrible that someone or something was for the country.

Donald J. Trump ✓ @realDonaldTrump · Apr 15, 2018

Slippery James Comey, a man who always ends up badly and out of whack (he is not smart!), will go down as the WORST FBI Director in history, by far!

Donald J. Trump ✓ @realDonaldTrump · Aug 18, 2018

Has anyone looked at the mistakes that John Brennan made while serving as CIA Director? He will go down as easily the WORST in history & since getting out, he has become nothing less than a loudmouth, partisan, political hack who cannot be trusted with the secrets to our country!

Donald J. Trump ✓ @realDonaldTrump · May 16, 2019

The Dems are getting another beauty to join their group. Bill de Blasio of NYC, considered the worst mayor in the U.S., will supposedly be making an announcement for president today. He is a JOKE, but if you like high taxes & crime, he's your man. NYC HATES HIM!

Donald J. Trump ✓ @realDonaldTrump · Sep 11, 2019

In a hypothetical poll, done by one of the worst pollsters of them all, the Amazon Washington Post/ABC, which predicted I would lose to Crooked Hillary by 15 points (how did that work out?), Sleepy Joe, Pocahontas and virtually all others would beat me in the General Election.

Donald J. Trump ✓ @realDonaldTrump · Dec 17, 2019

Good marks and reviews on the letter I sent to Pelosi today. She is the worst! No wonder with people like her and Cryin' Chuck Schumer, D.C. has been such a mess for so long - and that includes the previous administration who (and now we know for sure) SPIED on my campaign.

THE SO-CALLED

The president instilled doubt about the people who stood in the way of his agenda, either intentionally, through association, or simply by being in the wrong place at the wrong time, by referring to them on Twitter as "so-called." President Trump challenged their legitimacy outright, tweeting about so-called judges, whistleblowers, comedians, foreign leaders, and more.

Donald J. Trump @realDonaldTrump · Feb 4, 2017

The opinion of this so-called judge, which essentially takes law-enforcement away from our country, is ridiculous and will be overturned!

Donald J. Trump @realDonaldTrump · Feb 21, 2017

The so-called angry crowds in home districts of some Republicans are actually, in numerous cases, planned out by liberal activists. Sad!

Donald J. Trump @realDonaldTrump · Oct 25, 2018

The so-called experts on Trump over at the New York Times wrote a long and boring article on my cellphone usage that is so incorrect I do not have time here to correct it. I only use Government Phones, and have only one seldom used government cell phone. Story is soooo wrong!

Donald J. Trump @realDonaldTrump · Jan 17, 2020

The so-called "Supreme Leader" of Iran, who has not been so Supreme lately, had some nasty things to say about the United States and Europe. Their economy is crashing, and their people are suffering. He should be very careful with his words!

Donald J. Trump @realDonaldTrump · Feb 28, 2020

A so-called reporter named @JohnJHarwood, who bombed so badly in the 2016 Presidential Debates that I thought he was going to be immediately fired (a Mini Mike type performance), is now with Fake News @CNN. A total loser!

NICKNAMES, PUNS & INSULTS

The insulting nicknames that President Trump championed during his campaign and presidency — Crooked Hillary, Lyin' Ted, and Sleepy Joe Biden to name a few of the most popular ones — will likely live on long after the removal of the president's Twitter account. This collection of tweets highlights other classic insults like Senator Joe Munchkin (Manchin) and MSDNC (MSNBC).

Donald J. Trump @realDonaldTrump · Oct 10, 2017

The Failing @nytimes set Liddle' Bob Corker up by recording his conversation. Was made to sound a fool, and that's what I am dealing with!

Donald J. Trump @realDonaldTrump · Nov 19, 2017

Sen. Jeff Flake(y), who is unelectable in the Great State of Arizona (quit race, anemic polls) was caught (purposely) on "mike" saying bad things about your favorite President. He'll be a NO on tax cuts because his political career anyway is "toast."

Donald J. Trump @realDonaldTrump · Dec 2, 2019

Thank you to Great Republican @SenJohnKennedy for the job he did in representing both the Republican Party and myself against Sleepy Eyes Chuck Todd on Meet the Depressed!

Donald J. Trump @realDonaldTrump · Feb 9, 2020

They are really mad at Senator Joe Munchkin in West Virginia. He couldn't understand the Transcripts. Romney could, but didn't want to!

Donald J. Trump @realDonaldTrump · Apr 30, 2020

Lyin' Brian Williams of MSDNC, a Concast Scam Company, wouldn't know the truth if it was nailed to his wooden forehead. Remember when he lied about his bravery in a helicopter? Totally made up story. He's a true dummy who was thrown off Network News like a dog. Stay tuned!

TRUMP TWEETS ABOUT... THE HATERS
CELEBRITY FEUDS

Who called out Snoop Dogg, Oprah, Lebron James, Bette Midler, and more on Twitter while president? Donald J. Trump, of course! President Trump did not allow celebrity status to stop him from fighting back against his most famous critics. As soon as someone with a platform of their own took a public swipe at him, the president took to Twitter to share his opinion of their critique.

Donald J. Trump ✓ @realDonaldTrump · Mar 15, 2017

Can you imagine what the outcry would be if @SnoopDogg, failing career and all, had aimed and fired the gun at President Obama? Jail time!

Donald J. Trump ✓ @realDonaldTrump · Mar 31, 2017

Kathy Griffin should be ashamed of herself. My children, especially my 11 year old son, Barron, are having a hard time with this. Sick!

Donald J. Trump ✓ @realDonaldTrump · Dec 28, 2017

Vanity Fair, which looks like it is on its last legs, is bending over backwards in apologizing for the minor hit they took at Crooked H. Anna Wintour, who was all set to be Amb to Court of St James's & a big fundraiser for CH, is beside herself in grief & begging for forgiveness!

Donald J. Trump ✓ @realDonaldTrump · Feb 18, 2018

Just watched a very insecure Oprah Winfrey, who at one point I knew very well, interview a panel of people on 60 Minutes. The questions were biased and slanted, the facts incorrect. Hope Oprah runs so she can be exposed and defeated just like all of the others!

Donald J. Trump ✓ @realDonaldTrump · Mar 2, 2018

Alec Baldwin, whose dying mediocre career was saved by his terrible impersonation of me on SNL, now says playing me was agony. Alec, it was agony for those who were forced to watch. Bring back Darrell Hammond, funnier and a far greater talent!

MORE CELEBRITY FEUDS

The star-studded feuds that made the biggest headlines during President Trump's term in office included one with Kathy Griffin, who was quickly canceled after releasing a shocking photo of her holding the president's bloody, severed head in 2017, and another with Alec Baldwin, who impersonated the president in highly critical "Saturday Night Live" sketches for four years.

Donald J. Trump ✔ @realDonaldTrump · Jun 13, 2018

Robert De Niro, a very Low IQ individual, has received too many shots to the head by real boxers in movies. I watched him last night and truly believe he may be "punch-drunk." I guess he doesn't realize the economy is the best it's ever been with employment being at an all time high.

Donald J. Trump ✔ @realDonaldTrump · Jun 24, 2018

.@jimmyfallon is now whimpering to all that he did the famous "hair show" with me (where he seriously messed up my hair), & that he would have now done it differently because it is said to have "humanized" me-he is taking heat. He called & said "monster ratings." Be a man Jimmy!

Donald J. Trump ✔ @realDonaldTrump · Aug 3, 2018

Lebron James was just interviewed by the dumbest man on television, Don Lemon. He made Lebron look smart, which isn't easy to do. I like Mike!

Donald J. Trump ✔ @realDonaldTrump · Jun 4, 2019

Washed up psycho @BetteMidler was forced to apologize for a statement she attributed to me that turned out to be totally fabricated by her in order to make "your great president" look really bad. She got caught, just like the Fake News Media gets caught. A sick scammer!

Donald J. Trump ✔ @realDonaldTrump · Sep 5, 2019

Bad "actress" Debra The Mess Messing is in hot water. She wants to create a "Blacklist" of Trump supporters, & is being accused of McCarthyism. Is also being accused of being a Racist because of the terrible things she said about blacks and mental illness.

SOCIAL MEDIA GIANTS

Following the release of a 2018 Vice News article that accused Twitter of "shadow banning" prominent Republican users, President Trump echoed those allegations to his followers and promised to look into this "discriminatory and illegal practice at once!" The president continued this crusade against social media giants like Twitter and Facebook throughout the rest of his term.

Donald J. Trump ✔ @realDonaldTrump · Aug 18, 2018

Social Media is totally discriminating against Republican/Conservative voices. Speaking loudly and clearly for the Trump Administration, we won't let that happen. They are closing down the opinions of many people on the RIGHT, while at the same time doing nothing to others.

Donald J. Trump ✔ @realDonaldTrump · Aug 24, 2018

Social Media Giants are silencing millions of people. Can't do this even if it means we must continue to hear Fake News like CNN, whose ratings have suffered gravely. People have to figure out what is real, and what is not, without censorship!

Donald J. Trump ✔ @realDonaldTrump · Oct 26, 2018

Twitter has removed many people from my account and, more importantly, they have seemingly done something that makes it much harder to join - they have stifled growth to a point where it is obvious to all. A few weeks ago it was a Rocket Ship, now it is a Blimp! Total Bias?

Donald J. Trump ✔ @realDonaldTrump · May 3, 2019

The wonderful Diamond and Silk have been treated so horribly by Facebook. They work so hard and what has been done to them is very sad - and we're looking into. It's getting worse and worse for Conservatives on social media!

Donald J. Trump ✔ @realDonaldTrump · Jul 27, 2020

So disgusting to watch Twitter's so-called "Trending", where sooo many trends are about me, and never a good one. They look for anything they can find, make it as bad as possible, and blow it up, trying to make it trend. Really ridiculous, illegal, and, of course, very unfair!

During his re-election campaign, President Trump increased the frequency of his attacks on Big Tech, an umbrella term that encompassed both social media giants like Twitter and Facebook and influential multi-billion-dollar internet behemoths like Google, who the president accused without evidence of manipulating votes in the 2016 election and promoting negative articles about him.

Donald J. Trump ✅ @realDonaldTrump · Aug 28, 2018

Google search results for "Trump News" shows only the viewing/reporting of Fake News Media. In other words, they have it RIGGED, for me & others, so that almost all stories & news is BAD. Fake CNN is prominent. Republican/Conservative & Fair Media is shut out. Illegal?

Donald J. Trump ✅ @realDonaldTrump · May 27, 2020

Big Tech is doing everything in their very considerable power to CENSOR in advance of the 2020 Election. If that happens, we no longer have our freedom. I will never let it happen! They tried hard in 2016, and lost. Now they are going absolutely CRAZY. Stay Tuned!!!

Donald J. Trump ✅ @realDonaldTrump · Oct 28, 2020

It's amazing. Twitter refuses to allow the any mention of the Biden corruption story which was carried so well on @TuckerCarlson last night. It's the biggest story and Big Tech, together with the Lamestream Media, isn't allowing a word to be said about it.

Donald J. Trump ✅ @realDonaldTrump · Dec 1, 2020

Section 230, which is a liability shielding gift from the U.S. to "Big Tech" (the only companies in America that have it - corporate welfare!), is a serious threat to our National Security & Election Integrity. Our Country can never be safe & secure if we allow it to stand.

Donald J. Trump ✅ @realDonaldTrump · Dec 30, 2020

Twitter is shadow banning like never before. A disgrace that our weak and ineffective political leadership refuses to do anything about Big Tech. They're either afraid or stupid, nobody really knows!

THE REAL OPPOSITION PARTY

Ten days into his presidency, President Trump denounced the press as "the real opposition party." He later accused the media — generally understood to mean those well-known television news networks that consistently dedicated airtime to opinions critical of the president and his adminstration — of working secretly with the Democratic Party to obstruct his agenda.

Donald J. Trump ✓ @realDonaldTrump · Jan 30, 2017

Where was all the outrage from Democrats and the opposition party (the media) when our jobs were fleeing our country?

Donald J. Trump ✓ @realDonaldTrump · Jan 9, 2019

The Mainstream Media has NEVER been more dishonest than it is now. NBC and MSNBC are going Crazy. They report stories, purposely, the exact opposite of the facts. They are truly the Opposition Party working with the Dems. May even be worse than Fake News CNN, if that is possible!

Donald J. Trump ✓ @realDonaldTrump · Apr 10, 2020

Because the T.V. Ratings for the White House News Conference's are the highest, the Opposition Party (Lamestream Media), the Radical Left, Do Nothing Democrats &, of course, the few remaining RINO'S, are doing everything in their power to disparage & end them. The People's Voice!

Donald J. Trump ✓ @realDonaldTrump · Apr 12, 2020

The Opposition Party (Lamestream Media) and their partner, the Radical Left, Do Nothing Democrats, have put their political game plan in full swing. "Whether he is right or wrong, it doesn't matter. Criticize 'Trump' for everything, and don't let the public see Biden. Hide him."

Donald J. Trump ✓ @realDonaldTrump · Oct 7, 2020

THE FAKE NEWS MEDIA IS THE REAL OPPOSITION PARTY!

THE ENEMY OF THE PEOPLE

When using the phrase "enemy of the people" on Twitter, President Trump consistently stressed that he was referring not to all news outlets but to those he so often accused of publishing inaccurate or outright false information about his presidency. The fake news media are deserving of the title, he tweeted, because they intentionally sow distrust among the American people.

Donald J. Trump ✔ @realDonaldTrump · Feb 17, 2017

The FAKE NEWS media (failing @nytimes, @CNN, @NBCNews and many more) is not my enemy, it is the enemy of the American people. SICK!

Donald J. Trump ✔ @realDonaldTrump · Aug 5, 2018

The Fake News hates me saying that they are the Enemy of the People only because they know it's TRUE. I am providing a great service by explaining this to the American People. They purposely cause great division & distrust. They can also cause War! They are very dangerous & sick!

Donald J. Trump ✔ @realDonaldTrump · Nov 17, 2018

I can't imagine any President having a better or closer relationship with their Vice President then the two of us. Just more FAKE NEWS, the Enemy of the People!

Donald J. Trump ✔ @realDonaldTrump · Oct 29, 2018

There is great anger in our Country caused in part by inaccurate, and even fraudulent, reporting of the news. The Fake News Media, the true Enemy of the People, must stop the open & obvious hostility & report the news accurately & fairly. That will do much to put out the flame.

Donald J. Trump ✔ @realDonaldTrump · Dec 9, 2018

The Trump Administration has accomplished more than any other U.S. Administration in its first two (not even) years of existence, & we are having a great time doing it! All of this despite the Fake News Media, which has gone totally out of its mind-truly the Enemy of the People!

THE LAMESTREAM MEDIA

A highly successful purveyor of puns, President Trump introduced his 88.3 million Twitter followers to "lamestream media," a play on the phrase "mainstream media," in the summer of 2019. The president encouraged his supporters to distrust long-established television news networks like CNN and NBC by pairing the pun with accusations of dishonesty and corruption.

Donald J. Trump ✓ @realDonaldTrump · Aug 7, 2019

Watching Sleepy Joe Biden making a speech. Sooo Boring! The LameStream Media will die in the ratings and clicks with this guy. It will be over for them, not to mention the fact that our Country will do poorly with him. It will be one big crash, but at least China will be happy!

Donald J. Trump ✓ @realDonaldTrump · Aug 10, 2019

Never has the press been more inaccurate, unfair or corrupt! We are not fighting the Democrats, they are easy, we are fighting the seriously dishonest and unhinged Lamestream Media. They have gone totally CRAZY. MAKE AMERICA GREAT AGAIN!

Donald J. Trump ✓ @realDonaldTrump · Aug 16, 2019

Biggest crowd EVER, according to Arena people. Thousands outside trying to get in. Place was packed! Radical Left Dems & their Partner, LameStream Media, saying Arena empty. Check out pictures. Fake News. The Enemy of the People!

Donald J. Trump ✓ @realDonaldTrump · Aug 21, 2019

The Fake News LameStream Media is doing everything possible the "create" a U.S. recession, even though the numbers & facts are working totally in the opposite direction. They would be willing to hurt many people, but that doesn't matter to them. Our Economy is sooo strong, sorry!

Donald J. Trump ✓ @realDonaldTrump · Sep 2, 2019

The LameStream Media has gone totally CRAZY! They write whatever they want, seldom have sources (even though they say they do), never do "fact checking" anymore, and are only looking for the "kill." They take good news and make it bad. They are now beyond Fake, they are Corrupt.

FAKE NEWS!

President Trump tweeted about "fake news" more than 900 times during his four years in Washington. He lobbed the accusation at everything from reports about dysfunction within the White House and the alleged deterioration of his physical and mental health to descriptions of his crowd sizes at rallies and other events and the overall popularity of the Affordable Care Act.

Donald J. Trump @realDonaldTrump · Jan 18, 2017

Totally biased @NBCNews went out of its way to say that the big announcement from Ford, G.M., Lockheed & others that jobs are coming back to the U.S., but had nothing to do with TRUMP, is more FAKE NEWS. Ask top CEO's of those companies for real facts. Came back because of me!

Donald J. Trump @realDonaldTrump · Mar 15, 2017

Does anybody really believe that a reporter, who nobody ever heard of, "went to his mailbox" and found my tax returns? @NBCNews FAKE NEWS!

Donald J. Trump @realDonaldTrump · Dec 1, 2017

The media has been speculating that I fired Rex Tillerson or that he would be leaving soon - FAKE NEWS! He's not leaving and while we disagree on certain subjects, (I call the final shots) we work well together and America is highly respected again!

Donald J. Trump @realDonaldTrump · Dec 12, 2017

Despite thousands of hours wasted and many millions of dollars spent, the Democrats have been unable to show any collusion with Russia - so now they are moving on to the false accusations and fabricated stories of women who I don't know and/or have never met. FAKE NEWS!

Donald J. Trump @realDonaldTrump · Feb 20, 2018

I have been much tougher on Russia than Obama, just look at the facts. Total Fake News!

MORE FAKE NEWS

When it came to telling his side of the story, whether about a recent foreign policy decision or in response to the critical comments of an international celebrity, President Trump often chose to do so on Twitter. It was there on social media that he could speak directly to the American people without the added commentary or historical context often included by the mainstream media.

Donald J. Trump ✔ @realDonaldTrump · Feb 20, 2018

A woman I don't know and, to the best of my knowledge, never met, is on the FRONT PAGE of the Fake News Washington Post saying I kissed her (for two minutes yet) in the lobby of Trump Tower 12 years ago. Never happened! Who would do this in a public space with live security.

Donald J. Trump ✔ @realDonaldTrump · Apr 15, 2018

I never asked Comey for Personal Loyalty. I hardly even knew this guy. Just another of his many lies. His "memos" are self serving and FAKE!

Donald J. Trump ✔ @realDonaldTrump · Dec 24, 2018

I never "lashed out" at the Acting Attorney General of the U.S., a man for whom I have great respect. This is a made up story, one of many, by the Fake News Media!

Donald J. Trump ✔ @realDonaldTrump · Feb 19, 2019

I never said anything bad about Andrew McCabe's wife other than she (they) should not have taken large amounts of campaign money from a Crooked Hillary source when Clinton was under investigation by the FBI. I never called his wife a loser to him (another McCabe made up lie)!

Donald J. Trump ✔ @realDonaldTrump · Jun 2, 2019

I never called Meghan Markle "nasty." Made up by the Fake News Media, and they got caught cold! Will @CNN, @nytimes and others apologize? Doubt it!

EVEN MORE FAKE NEWS!

A Pew Research Center study of the media coverage of President Trump's first 60 days in office found that he received far more negative news coverage than former Presidents Obama, Bush, and Clinton. A whopping 60% of the news stories studied gave an overall negative assessment of the president's words or actions while only 33% of stories were deemed neutral in their coverage.

Donald J. Trump ✔ @realDonaldTrump · Aug 26, 2019

The story by Axios that President Trump wanted to blow up large hurricanes with nuclear weapons prior to reaching shore is ridiculous. I never said this. Just more FAKE NEWS!

Donald J. Trump ✔ @realDonaldTrump · Nov 7, 2019

The degenerate Washington Post MADE UP the story about me asking Bill Barr to hold a news conference. Never happened, and there were no sources!

Donald J. Trump ✔ @realDonaldTrump · Dec 1, 2019

The Fake News said I played golf today, and I did NOT! I had meeting in various locations, while closely monitoring the U.S. Embassy situation in Iraq, which I am still doing. The Corrupt Lamestream Media knew this but, not surprisingly, failed to report or correct!

Donald J. Trump ✔ @realDonaldTrump · Apr 25, 2020

I never said the pandemic was a Hoax! Who would say such a thing? I said that the Do Nothing Democrats, together with their Mainstream Media partners, are the Hoax. They have been called out & embarrassed on this, even admitting they were wrong, but continue to spread the lie!

Donald J. Trump ✔ @realDonaldTrump · Nov 25, 2020

The "losers & suckers" statement on dead military heroes has been proven to be a total fabrication and lie. IT WAS NEVER MADE! The "anonymous" fabricator, who is a major sleaze, went forward with the lie despite 25 strong witnesses to the contrary. Welcome to the roaring 20's!

THE AMAZON WASHINGTON POST

President Trump was no fan of the Washington Post, a newspaper purchased in 2013 by Amazon CEO and multi-billionaire Jeff Bezos. He occasionally took to Twitter to accuse the newspaper of acting as a "lobbyist" or "propaganda machine" for Amazon, especially when the paper won Pulitzer prizes for its work or released polls predicting the president would lose the 2020 election.

Donald J. Trump ✔ @realDonaldTrump · Jul 23, 2017

It's hard to read the Failing New York Times or the Amazon Washington Post because every story/opinion, even if should be positive, is bad!

Donald J. Trump ✔ @realDonaldTrump · Jul 24, 2017

Is Fake News Washington Post being used as a lobbyist weapon against Congress to keep Politicians from looking into Amazon no-tax monopoly?

Donald J. Trump ✔ @realDonaldTrump · Jul 7, 2018

Twitter is getting rid of fake accounts at a record pace. Will that include the Failing New York Times and propaganda machine for Amazon, the Washington Post, who constantly quote anonymous sources that, in my opinion, don't exist - They will both be out of business in 7 years!

Donald J. Trump ✔ @realDonaldTrump · Jan 13, 2019

So sorry to hear the news about Jeff Bozo being taken down by a competitor whose reporting, I understand, is far more accurate than the reporting in his lobbyist newspaper, the Amazon Washington Post. Hopefully the paper will soon be placed in better & more responsible hands!

Donald J. Trump ✔ @realDonaldTrump · Jun 16, 2019

A poll should be done on which is the more dishonest and deceitful newspaper, the Failing New York Times or the Amazon (lobbyist) Washington Post! They are both a disgrace to our Country, the Enemy of the People, but I just can't seem to figure out which is worse?

THE FAILING NEW YORK TIMES

President Trump's signature criticism of the New York Times, the newspaper that currently holds the record for being awarded the most Pulitzer prizes in journalism, was its slowing subscription rates and low ad revenue, hence "the failing New York Times." President Trump often attacked the NYT for relying on anonymous sources, a practice used to protect people from retribution.

Donald J. Trump ✔ @realDonaldTrump · Jan 28, 2017

The failing @nytimes has been wrong about me from the very beginning. Said I would lose the primaries, then the general election. FAKE NEWS!

Donald J. Trump ✔ @realDonaldTrump · May 26, 2018

Unlike what the Failing and Corrupt New York Times would like people to believe, there is ZERO disagreement within the Trump Administration as to how to deal with North Korea and if there was, it wouldn't matter. The @nytimes has called me wrong right from the beginning!

Donald J. Trump ✔ @realDonaldTrump · Sep 5, 2018

Does the so-called "Senior Administration Official" really exist, or is it just the Failing New York Times with another phony source? If the GUTLESS anonymous person does indeed exist, the Times must, for National Security purposes, turn him/her over to government at once!

Donald J. Trump ✔ @realDonaldTrump · Aug 15, 2019

Wow! The Deputy Editor of the Failing New York Times was just demoted. Should have been Fired! Totally biased and inaccurate reporting. The paper is a Fraud, Zero Credibility. Fake News takes another hit, but this time a big one!

Donald J. Trump ✔ @realDonaldTrump · Sep 16, 2019

I call for the Resignation of everybody at The New York Times involved in the Kavanaugh SMEAR story, and while you're at it, the Russian Witch Hunt Hoax, which is just as phony! They've taken the Old Grey Lady and broken her down, destroyed her virtue and ruined her reputation.

FAKE NEWS CNN

Throughout his campaign and presidency, President Trump appeared to loathe no television news network more than CNN. He regularly taunted the network about its ratings and accused its journalists of reporting inaccurate stories solely because they portrayed the president in a negative light. President Trump put CNN on Twitter blast for the final time on December 30, 2020.

Donald J. Trump ✔ @realDonaldTrump · Jan 24, 2017

Congratulations to @FoxNews for being number one in inauguration ratings. They were many times higher than FAKE NEWS @CNN - public is smart!

Donald J. Trump ✔ @realDonaldTrump · Nov 27, 2017

We should have a contest as to which of the Networks, plus CNN and not including Fox, is the most dishonest, corrupt and/or distorted in its political coverage of your favorite President (me). They are all bad. Winner to receive the FAKE NEWS TROPHY!

Donald J. Trump ✔ @realDonaldTrump · Dec 9, 2017

CNN'S slogan is CNN, THE MOST TRUSTED NAME IN NEWS. Everyone knows this is not true, that this could, in fact, be a fraud on the American Public. There are many outlets that are far more trusted than Fake News CNN. Their slogan should be CNN, THE LEAST TRUSTED NAME IN NEWS!

Donald J. Trump ✔ @realDonaldTrump · Mar 26, 2019

The Fake News Media has lost tremendous credibility with its corrupt coverage of the illegal Democrat Witch Hunt of your all time favorite duly elected President, me! T.V. ratings of CNN & MSNBC tanked last night after seeing the Mueller Report statement. @FoxNews up BIG!

Donald J. Trump ✔ @realDonaldTrump · Mar 25, 2020

I hear that Fake News CNN just reported that I am isolated in the White House, wondering out loud, "when will life return to normal?" Does anybody really believe that? There was no leak, they made it up – they are CORRUPT & FAKE NEWS.

WHAT'S WITH FOX NEWS?

When President Trump interpreted Fox News' coverage of his words or actions to be positive, he applauded the network for its journalistic integrity. When the coverage was less pleasant, however, he lashed out against the network on Twitter. Despite the president's many criticisms, Fox News remained the most-watched cable news network during every year of his presidency.

Donald J. Trump ✔ @realDonaldTrump · Apr 16, 2019

Many Trump Fans & Signs were outside of the @FoxNews Studio last night in the now thriving (Thank you President Trump) Bethlehem, Pennsylvania, for the interview with Crazy Bernie Sanders. Big complaints about not being let in-stuffed with Bernie supporters. What's with @FoxNews?

Donald J. Trump ✔ @realDonaldTrump · Aug 28, 2019

I don't want to Win for myself, I only want to Win for the people. The New @FoxNews is letting millions of GREAT people down! We have to start looking for a new News Outlet. Fox isn't working for us anymore!

Donald J. Trump ✔ @realDonaldTrump · Nov 17, 2019

.@SteveScalise blew the nasty & obnoxious Chris Wallace (will never be his father, Mike!) away on Chris's lowest rated (unless I'm on) morning show. This kind of dumb and unfair interview would never have happened in the @FoxNews past. Great job Steve!

Donald J. Trump ✔ @realDonaldTrump · Oct 22, 2020

.@FoxNews Polls are totally FAKE, just like they were in 2016. I am leading in all of the states mentioned, which you will soon see. I thought Fox was getting rid of its pollster. Sadly, it never happened!

Donald J. Trump ✔ @realDonaldTrump · Dec 16, 2020

Can't believe how badly @FoxNews is doing in the ratings. They played right into the hands of the Radical Left Democrats, & now are floating in limboland. Hiring fired @donnabrazile, and far worse, allowing endless negative and unedited commercials. @FoxNews is dead. Really Sad!

WE ALL MISS ROGER AILES

One of the ways President Trump criticized Fox News was to recall the cable news network's former CEO Roger Ailes, who researchers credit for pretty much single-handedly transforming Fox News into the most-watched cable news network in America. The president lamented that the network had changed after Ailes' resignation in 2016 amid allegations of sexual harassment.

Donald J. Trump ✓ @realDonaldTrump · May 18, 2020

.@FoxNews is no longer the same. We miss the great Roger Ailes. You have more anti-Trump people, by far, than ever before. Looking for a new outlet!

Donald J. Trump ✓ @realDonaldTrump · May 22, 2020

Why doesn't @FoxNews put up the CNBC POLL or the (believe it or not!) @CNN Poll? Hope Roger A is looking down and watching what has happened to this once beautiful creation!

Donald J. Trump ✓ @realDonaldTrump · Jun 30, 2020

She gets fired by @CNN for giving Crooked Hillary the debate questions, and gets hired by @FoxNews. Where are you Roger Ailes?

Donald J. Trump ✓ @realDonaldTrump · Jun 30, 2020

I know better than anyone that my friend Roger Ailes died 3 years ago, just look at what happened to @FoxNews. We all miss Roger!!!

Donald J. Trump ✓ @realDonaldTrump · Oct 12, 2020

.@FoxNews allows more negative ads on me than practically all of the other networks combined. Not like the old days, but we will win even bigger than 2016. Roger Ailes was the GREATEST!

RETURN THE PULITZERS!

The 2018 Pulitzer Prize in National Reporting was awarded to the staffs of the New York Times and Washington Post for articles written about the investigation into Russian attempts to interfere with the 2016 election. President Trump made his disapproval known via tweet, claiming, despite evidence to the contrary, that the articles were false and calling for the prizes to be revoked.

Donald J. Trump ✓ @realDonaldTrump · Mar 29, 2019

So funny that The New York Times & The Washington Post got a Pulitzer Prize for their coverage (100% NEGATIVE and FAKE!) of Collusion with Russia - And there was No Collusion! So, they were either duped or corrupt? In any event, their prizes should be taken away by the Committee!

Donald J. Trump ✓ @realDonaldTrump · May 10, 2020

When are the Fake Journalists, who received unwarranted Pulitzer Prizes for Russia, Russia, Russia, and the Impeachment Scam, going to turn in their tarnished awards so they can be given to the real journalists who got it right. I'll give you the names, there are plenty of them!

Donald J. Trump ✓ @realDonaldTrump · May 26, 2020

The Failing @nytimes, winner of @PulitzerPrizes for its totally flawed coverage of the illegal Russia Witch Hunt, does its research as follows: Think of the absolute worst things you can say about Donald J. Trump, pretend there are sources, and just say it. RETURN THE PULITZERS!

Donald J. Trump ✓ @realDonaldTrump · Jul 4, 2020

Sara, the Silent Majority will speak on NOVEMBER 3rd. You are doing a Great job &, together with some very well known others who got it right on Russia, Russia, Russia, should get a now very discredited Pulitzer Prize. Committee should get them back from those that got it wrong!

Donald J. Trump ✓ @realDonaldTrump · Jul 11, 2020

John, among others, should have gotten a Pulitzer for exposing Russia, Russia, Russia as Fake News. He was right. The "journalists" who got them were all WRONG. Take back the Pulitzers, which have become a JOKE!

THIRD-RATE REPORTERS

President Trump's relationship with reporters was contentious both online and off. From the White House briefing room to his preferred social media platform, the president routinely berated individual journalists for their coverage of his time in the Oval Office. Those journalists often wrote critically about the Trump administration and were dubbed "third-rate" by the Twitterer-in-Chief.

Donald J. Trump ✔ @realDonaldTrump · Apr 21, 2018

The New York Times and a third rate reporter named Maggie Haberman, known as a Crooked H flunkie who I don't speak to and have nothing to do with, are going out of their way to destroy Michael Cohen and his relationship with me in the hope that he will "flip."

Donald J. Trump ✔ @realDonaldTrump · Jan 18, 2020

Another Fake Book by two third rate Washington Post reporters, has already proven to be inaccurately reported, to their great embarrassment, all for the purpose of demeaning and belittling a President who is getting great things done for our Country, at a record clip. Thank you!

Donald J. Trump ✔ @realDonaldTrump · Mar 11, 2020

Vanity Fair Magazine, which will soon be out of business, and their third rate Fake reporters, who make up sources which don't exist, wrote yet another phony & boring hit piece. The facts are just the opposite. Our team is doing a great job with CoronaVirus!

Donald J. Trump ✔ @realDonaldTrump · Mar 27, 2020

She is a third rate reporter who has nothing going. A Fake News "journalist".

Donald J. Trump ✔ @realDonaldTrump · Apr 26, 2020

I read a phony story in the failing @nytimes about my work schedule and eating habits, written by a third rate reporter who knows nothing about me. I will often be in the Oval Office late into the night & read & see that I am angrily eating a hamburger & Diet Coke in my bedroom. People with me are always stunned.

FREEDOM OF THE PRESS

Freedom of the press has been regarded as a cornerstone of American democracy since the country's earliest days but even Founding Father Thomas Jefferson took issue with the press back in his day. He wrote in one letter, "I deplore... the putrid state into which our newspapers have passed and the malignity, the vulgarity, and mendacious spirit of those who write for them."

Donald J. Trump ✔ @realDonaldTrump · Jul 29, 2018

When the media - driven insane by their Trump Derangement Syndrome - reveals internal deliberations of our government, it truly puts the lives of many, not just journalists, at risk! Very unpatriotic! Freedom of the press also comes with a responsibility to report the news.

Donald J. Trump ✔ @realDonaldTrump · Aug 16, 2018

There is nothing that I would want more for our Country than true FREEDOM OF THE PRESS. The fact is that the Press is FREE to write and say anything it wants, but much of what it says is FAKE NEWS, pushing a political agenda or just plain trying to hurt people. HONESTY WINS!

Donald J. Trump ✔ @realDonaldTrump · Nov 7, 2019

Bill Barr did not decline my request to talk about Ukraine. The story was a Fake Washington Post con job with an "anonymous" source that doesn't exist. Just read the Transcript. The Justice Department already ruled that the call was good. We don't have freedom of the press!

Donald J. Trump ✔ @realDonaldTrump · Oct 28, 2020

The USA doesn't have Freedom of the Press, we have Suppression of the Story, or just plain Fake News. So much has been learned in the last two weeks about how corrupt our Media is, and now Big Tech, maybe even worse. Repeal Section 230!

Donald J. Trump ✔ @realDonaldTrump · Nov 27, 2020

Big Tech and the Fake News Media have partnered to Suppress. Freedom of the Press is gone, a thing of the past. That's why they refuse to report the real facts and figures of the 2020 Election or even, where's Hunter!

FREE SPEECH

In the second half of his presidency, President Trump stoked the flames of rising concern among conservative Twitter users when he tweeted that the social media giant (and privately owned American company) was stifling free speech. After getting banned from Twitter himself, the president announced that he'd be launching his own social media platform called Truth Social.

Donald J. Trump ✓ @realDonaldTrump · Jul 25, 2017

If U.C. Berkeley does not allow free speech and practices violence on innocent people with a different point of view - NO FEDERAL FUNDS?

Donald J. Trump ✓ @realDonaldTrump · May 3, 2019

I am continuing to monitor the censorship of AMERICAN CITIZENS on social media platforms. This is the United States of America — and we have what's known as FREEDOM OF SPEECH! We are monitoring and watching, closely!!

Donald J. Trump ✓ @realDonaldTrump · Oct 8, 2019

Someone please tell the Radical Left Mayor of Minneapolis that he can't price out Free Speech. Probably illegal! I stand strongly & proudly with the great Police Officers and Law Enforcement of Minneapolis and the Great State of Minnesota! See you Thursday Night!

Donald J. Trump ✓ @realDonaldTrump · May 26, 2020

Twitter is completely stifling FREE SPEECH, and I, as President, will not allow it to happen!

Donald J. Trump ✓ @realDonaldTrump · Dec 24, 2020

Twitter is going wild with their flags, trying hard to suppress even the truth. Just shows how dangerous they are, purposely stifling free speech. Very dangerous for our Country. Does Congress know that this is how Communism starts? Cancel Culture at its worst. End Section 230!

VERY LOW RATINGS

CNN wasn't the only television news network that President Trump used low ratings to criticize. The president took a bipartisan approach with his Twitter attacks, lashing out at right- and left-leaning news outlets alike. Even Fox News, home to some of the president's most vocally supportive news anchors, did not escape the president's ratings criticisms on social media.

Donald J. Trump @realDonaldTrump · Oct 4, 2017

NBC news is #FakeNews and more dishonest than even CNN. They are a disgrace to good reporting. No wonder their news ratings are way down!

Donald J. Trump @realDonaldTrump · Jul 31, 2018

The Fake News Media is going CRAZY! They are totally unhinged and in many ways, after witnessing first hand the damage they do to so many innocent and decent people, I enjoy watching. In 7 years, when I am no longer in office, their ratings will dry up and they will be gone!

Donald J. Trump @realDonaldTrump · Feb 26, 2020

Low Ratings Fake News MSDNC (Comcast) & @CNN are doing everything possible to make the Caronavirus look as bad as possible, including panicking markets, if possible. Likewise their incompetent Do Nothing Democrat comrades are all talk, no action. USA in great shape!

Donald J. Trump @realDonaldTrump · Oct 13, 2020

Congratulations Dan. You, Breitbart and others have decimated the business at Drudge. It's gone the way of the @NBA, ratings down 70%. People want the TRUTH! Drudge Report sold out, suffered a massive "nervous breakdown". Happening @FoxNews also???

Donald J. Trump @realDonaldTrump · Nov 12, 2020

.@FoxNews daytime ratings have completely collapsed. Weekend daytime even WORSE. Very sad to watch this happen, but they forgot what made them successful, what got them there. They forgot the Golden Goose. The biggest difference between the 2016 Election, and 2020, was @FoxNews!

TRUMP TWEETS

Donald J. Trump ✔
@realDonaldTrump

A tremendous **WORD SEARCH BOOK** for adults -- even the haters and losers!

10:23 PM · May 7, 2020 from The White House · Twitter for iPhone

VOLUME 1: TWITTERER-IN-CHIEF

NOT A FAN

Donald J. Trump ✔
@realDonaldTrump

Phoenix crowd last night was amazing - a packed house. I love the Great State of Arizona. Not a fan of Jeff Flake, weak on crime & border!
9:20 AM · Aug 23, 2017

Reason I canceled my trip to London is that I am not a big fan of the Obama Administration having sold perhaps the best located and finest embassy in London for "peanuts," only to build a new one in an off location for 1.2 billion dollars. Bad deal. Wanted me to cut ribbon-NO!
11:57 PM · Jan 11, 2018

Had a great meeting with the House GOP last night at the Capitol. They applauded and laughed loudly when I mentioned my experience with Mark Sanford. I have never been a fan of his!
4:04 PM · Jun 20, 2018

Never a fan of @justinamash, a total lightweight who opposes me and some of our great Republican ideas and policies just for the sake of getting his name out there through controversy. If he actually read the biased Mueller Report, "composed" by 18 Angry Dems who hated Trump.
9:55 AM · May 19, 2019

I am not a fan of Bitcoin and other Cryptocurrencies, which are not money, and whose value is highly volatile and based on thin air. Unregulated Crypto Assets can facilitate unlawful behavior, including drug trade and other illegal activity.
8:15 PM · Jul 11, 2019

```
A R I Z O L L A R L U F W A L N U O
P P A P P L A U D E D Z O E A R I Z
P H O E N C I X E D R A N U R E O N
L O P A T R I P I E B A M L K T H I
A E H S S Y E M L H A V I A T H N U
B N X F B P H D L G O R L V Z A X N
E I A H E T L R E U G F L A K I E R
H N O D N O L U G A R I Z O N A N E
A R I Z S C E G A L A W F E L O D G
V E F N A U Z M L I E V O L O B O U
I L A I R R S R B N G H D O N I N L
O I B H N R B I B A P E A N U T S A
R T I T A E I B O K S S P E A C U T
A A T L P N S B N E T S U N R O G E
I L L T R C O T B E S T Y O R I U D
N O I L L I B A S O R I B B E N L O
D V F A C E L S D O N O L L A R A L
P H O E N S A F A C I L I T A T E L
```

PHOENIX	EMBASSY	CRYPTOCURRENCIES
AMAZING	PEANUTS	THIN
LOVE	BILLION	AIR
ARIZONA	DOLLARS	UNREGULATED
FLAKE	RIBBON	ASSETS
TRIP	APPLAUDED	FACILITATE
LONDON	LAUGHED	UNLAWFUL
FAN	BITCOIN	BEHAVIOR
SOLD	VALUE	DRUG
FINEST	VOLATILE	ILLEGAL

3d685484-38b4-4a50-a67b-fed52588cc01R01